THE BASIS OF BELIEF

IS VOLUME

13

OF THE

Twentieth Century Encyclopedia of Catholicism

UNDER SECTION

I

KNOWLEDGE AND FAITH

IT IS ALSO THE

59TH

VOLUME IN ORDER OF PUBLICATION

Edited by HENRI DANIEL-ROPS *of the* Académie Française

THE BASIS OF BELIEF

By ILLTYD TRETHOWAN, O.S.B.

57596

HAWTHORN BOOKS · PUBLISHERS · *New York*

First Edition, February, 1961

NIHIL OBSTAT

Carolus Davis, S.T.L.

Censor Deputatus

IMPRIMATUR

E. Morrogh Bernard

Vicarius Generalis

Westmonasterii, die XXVIII NOVEMBRIS MCMLX

CONTENTS

INTRODUCTION

This book must begin with a warning. Anyone who wants to find a Catholic "party-line" about the philosophy of religion must look for it elsewhere—not that there is such a thing as a Catholic "party-line" if we mean by this a line which Catholics are bound to follow, but there are more usual and less usual approaches to the subject. This is one of the less usual.

The Church does not teach a philosophical system, but Christianity does provide answers to certain philosophical problems, notably that of God's existence, and it does imply certain philosophical conclusions, notably in regard to man's nature—his free will, for example. Within these limits, Catholics are free to adopt any philosophical system or none. At various times various philosophical systems have been popular among them, and in our time most Catholic thinkers are Thomists, that is, they accept, at least in its broad outlines, the Aristotelian system adopted and to some extent transformed by St Thomas Aquinas. St Thomas was a theologian, and he was interested in philosophy, quite rightly, only because of its importance for religion. He is the Church's official theologian in the sense that his conclusions have been incorporated in many cases into the Church's teaching, and his authority is paramount. But St Thomas is not infallible as a theologian or as a philosopher. The Church insists that her future priests shall be instructed in Thomism, and there are obvious advantages in such an arrangement. There is no obligation to accept Thomism as a system.

The usual approach, then, to the philosophy of religion, for Catholics, is by way of Thomist psychology and metaphysics. Some people cannot make much of these doctrines, and some people find them, in a greater or a lesser degree, unsatisfactory. Such persons may perhaps find a less usual approach more helpful, especially if, like the present one, it does not require an array of technical terms, metaphysical notions and piled-up syllogisms. One unusual approach has already been indicated in this series by Canon Nédoncelle in *Is There a Christian Philosophy?*; indeed it resembles the present one very closely on the central topic, which is the affirmation of God. But Canon Nédoncelle, whose treatment was largely historical (apart from the special question about the relation between philosophy and theology which was his immediate concern), could do no more than indicate such an approach in the space provided for him. And he did not write his book for an English-speaking public, which has very special requirements.

The philosophy of religion has had a bad press for the last thirty years or so in the English-speaking countries. Academic philosophers have been, on the whole, hostile or indifferent to it, and many convinced Christians, influenced principally by Karl Barth, have given it up as a bad job. Even among Catholics a form of anti-intellectualism, more sophisticated and elusive than the nineteenth-century variety, has been observable. This particular phenomenon has been due to the discredit into which metaphysics has fallen during the period. Now that a more balanced view is becoming fashionable, it is to be hoped that a reasonable distrust of metaphysical systems will no longer lead to the rejection, out of hand, of all metaphysical doctrines, that is, to put it as shortly as possible, of philosophical doctrines according to which there is more in life than meets the eye. The philosophy of religion, in the form in which it will be recommended here, is not a way of complicating religion for believers; it is concerned principally with unbelievers and endeavours to remove certain apparent obstacles to belief in God. It seems reasonable to hold that the removal of such obstacles is the chief duty of charity laid upon Christians today.

There is nothing substantive in these pages which I have not already offered to the public elsewhere. This is simply an attempt to say what I have to say in a more useful form, with some discussion of recent work on the subject and of the criticisms which my previous writings have encountered. I know that many will disagree with me, and I shall be content if I can contribute, in however small a way, to keep the debate alive.

The editor of *The Tablet* has kindly authorized me to use in this book materials which first appeared in his pages.

CHAPTER I

AN UNPOPULAR SUBJECT

"The philosophy of religion" is a phrase which has nowadays an old-fashioned ring about it. There was a great deal of writing in the nineteenth century which described itself in those terms and which was, in the eyes of most of us today, very vague and unsatisfactory. It is perhaps for that reason that contemporary writers in this field have preferred to speak of the "philosophy of theism". It might be urged, too, that there is a difference in meaning between the two expressions: "religion" is a wider term than "theism" and covers beliefs of many kinds—polytheism, for example, and belief in an impersonal power at the back of things. Nevertheless, I have preferred to avoid the more technical phrase, partly because this is not (in my intention, at least) a technical book, partly because "religion", in our society, has always meant, and (outside certain highly sophisticated circles) continues to mean, a belief in one God who created the world, who is different from the world, perfect and infinite, and who demands our worship and our service. At any rate, that is what it means in this book.

THE FUNCTION OF THE PHILOSOPHY OF RELIGION

But it is not only this particular form of words which has come to seem old-fashioned to so many people; the subject itself has become unfashionable even in the least expected quarters. It is not surprising, in view of the prevailing intellectual climate, that modern philosophers generally should have no great interest in it; but it is surprising that it should be so often disregarded by Christian thinkers, Catholics included. This is a state of affairs which obviously demands investigation at the outset.

It is, of course, perfectly natural and in order that Catholics should regard the philosophy of religion as a subject which does not directly concern their own lives as religious men. They have the answers to the questions which the philosophers of religion discuss so ineffectually. But what about their less fortunate friends who are still grappling with—or avoiding—these questions? Do they not require help on the philosophical level? No, it will be said, that is a waste of time. God has revealed himself in Christ and it is in Christ, in Christ's Mystical Body the Church, that he is to be found. Belief in God, solid and genuine belief, goes hand in hand with institutional religion and is hardly found apart from it; this is a matter of history. Christianity brings deliverance from the interminable debates of the philosophers. Let us not, then, entangle our friends in arguments, but try to make them realize that it is a *fact* which really matters, the fact of Christ. They must read the Bible, and come to Mass. God will do the rest.

The only trouble about this programme is that it will not always work. If it does, then it would be indeed a waste of time to insist on philosophical preliminaries (although if the truths of Christianity are to be properly understood the sort of thinking which philosophers do cannot be avoided altogether). The question about religion is indeed not one of theorizing, but of fact, as Abbot Butler has recently shown with great clarity and energy in *Why Christ?*[1] But at the end of the book he refers to "the invitation of God implicit in all human experience",[2] and that is where the philosophy of religion comes in. For it is the widespread failure to acknowledge this invitation which holds things up. There are so many people about who have no interest in religion and who cannot be persuaded to take any interest in it because their human experience is, in certain all-important respects, in a state of

[1] Darton, Longman and Todd and Helicon Press, 1960.
[2] *Op. cit.*, p. 161.

arrested development. And it is the philosophy of religion which must be brought to bear on this situation.

CATHOLICISM AND THE PHILOSOPHY OF RELIGION

If that is so, then, although the subject remains unnecessary in theory for the spiritual well-being of a Catholic, it proves to be of such supreme importance for an understanding of the human situation that in practice a lack of interest in it would be somewhat disquieting: there would seem to be a certain deficiency, a failure to grasp the full truth about oneself, quite apart from any question of helping others. But the suggestion that it is the business of philosophy, even of the philosophy of religion, to explore neglected areas of human experience encounters a good deal of disapproval among Catholics. Those who have studied philosophy at a University in the English-speaking world during the past thirty years or so sometimes object that philosophy is fundamentally an affair of logic. People continue to insist that they have no knowledge of God which is not derived from the Bible (this has been said to me by a Catholic who is also a professional philosopher). And some will say that the Church has made declarations about man's natural knowledge of God which they find puzzling but which they do not wish to traverse—and that the present suggestion, if it is not too vague to mean anything, does traverse them.

It is impossible to give quick answers to these objections. But I hope that the answers which I have to offer will emerge clearly enough as the book proceeds. Something, however, should be said at once about the Church's teaching on our subject, for it has been often misconceived. The facts are simple. The Vatican Council laid it down, in this simply re-affirming the Church's teaching, that the one true God, our Creator and Lord, can be certainly known in the light of natural reason through the things which are made; to this the anti-modernist oath added the phrase "as cause and effect" and reinforced "certainly known" by the further addition "and also demonstrated". There have been two extreme views about the significance of these pronouncements. On the one hand, it has been said that they do not really commit Catholic philosophers to anything, since nothing is laid down about the capacity of anyone in particular to know that God exists by the exercise of his natural powers. To say that it *can* be done is not even to say that anybody has yet succeeded in doing it, only that somebody could do so in unspecified circumstances. Thus if we find ourselves unable to do so we need not worry. The anti-modernist oath is not infallible, the argument continues, and the less said about it the better. The other extreme view is that Catholics are committed here and now to the defence of a purely logical proof of God's existence.

It may be fairly obvious that the first of these views in effect evacuates the pronouncements of any real significance, and that the second reads too much into them. We must make sure of this by examining the general content of the pronouncements. They prove, as we should expect, not to be concerned with any particular philosophical theories about proving God's existence but with the theological fact that all men are summoned by God to a supernatural destiny. Many are ignorant, through no fault of their own, that God has revealed himself to men in Jesus Christ. But they cannot fail to attain salvation through no fault of their own. If they do what is in them, if they follow such lights as they have, God will not reject them. This is the doctrine of "baptism by desire" on which the Church has found it necessary to insist more than once in the recent past. The Vatican Council, then, was insisting that all men must have the opportunity of acknowledging God's existence even if they are ignorant of Revelation. The error which was envisaged was that of the "traditionalists" according to whom there could be no knowledge of God without belief in Revelation.

We cannot, therefore, reduce the significance of these pronouncements to the assertion of a mere abstract possibility. What is at stake is a practical question of supreme importance.

All men must come before God as their Judge, and so they must be able to make that choice on which their destiny depends. They must have a knowledge of God which will make that choice possible. It may be only an "implicit" knowledge— they may not realize that by "doing what is in them", that is, by following the dictates of their conscience, they are in fact acknowledging God's claims upon them. But this is sufficient, and necessary. At the same time, it becomes clear that a knowledge of God "in the light of human reason through the things which are made" does not imply anything which we should normally call an "argument" at all. There might be arguments available, but nothing is said about them here. The reference to "the things which are made" is a reference to St Paul's words in the Epistle to the Romans (1. 20), and means no more than that men may discover God's existence by considering the world of his creation. It is for the philosophy of religion to consider how they do it.

The anti-modernist oath is not to be interpreted as going beyond the decisions of the Council in adding the phrase "as cause by effect"; there is still no reference to a particular form of argument. And its use of the word "demonstrated" cannot be made to bear any technical significance. As it stands, it means no more than that evidence for God's existence can be "pointed out" or shown to those who do not acknowledge it. Here again the context of the declaration is decisive. The oath is concerned with the anti-intellectual position of modernists who regarded religious conviction as a matter of "feeling" to which rational discourse is irrelevant. What is laid down, there-fore, in the oath is that we can appeal to common ground in a discussion with professing atheists or agnostics. They are capable of perceiving the truth of God's existence in so far as they have human powers of intelligence.

IS THERE A "NATURAL" KNOWLEDGE OF GOD?

It is often emphasized nowadays that these human powers may be assisted by God's grace at any stage. Before a man receives sanctifying grace, by the sacrament of baptism or by baptism of desire, he may receive special help from God. And it is sometimes urged, at the same time, that the unaided powers of human reason need not be expected to provide more than a very vague and ineffectual awareness of God's existence. All this may be admitted, but it does not seem to affect the real issue. The distinction with which we are concerned is the distinction between the knowledge of God which is possible without knowledge of the Christian Revelation and the knowledge of God which that Revelation supplies. It could be that our native endowment of intelligence is always too feeble to provide us with an effective knowledge of God, that it always requires supplementation by God's special graces, but in that case we must suppose that these graces are in fact always supplied. All knowledge of God must be, in a broad sense, God's self-revelation and the possible modes of this revelation are beyond our inquiry. Somehow or other, in any case, those who are ignorant of the Christian Revelation must be enabled to choose God: they must have a knowledge which is effective for that purpose, and our business is to consider the characteristics of that knowledge and the means of promoting it. We want to discover what is common to all men in this matter, whether they have knowledge of the Christian Revelation or not. It may be that our original powers are always helped by "special grace", but our previous conclusion still imposes itself: a knowledge of God is available for all men, previous to the acceptance of Christianity.

But if a supplementation of nature by grace is required by some men, or by all men, before they acquire that knowledge which must be, somehow and sometime, common to them all, the question arises whether the philosophy of religion, if it has to take account of God's grace, is properly so-called; for the philosopher is usually supposed to be concerned with nature and not with grace. To this it might be replied that there is no better name for this field of inquiry, that if the philosophy of religion seems to be a misleading description of it, any other description will be still more misleading: "fundamental theology" is used in another meaning, and "natural theology" implies the exclusion of grace in a more obvious way. But in any case the objection is an artificial one. To say that there is no "philosophical" or "natural" knowledge of God, on the ground that our native powers of intelligence are supplemented by "grace," is to use the word grace in an inappropriate sense; if it is something with which everybody *has* to be supplied in order that he may be enabled to "choose God" it would be better to call it a perfecting of the natural endowment. For the sphere of grace is that of freedom, whereas the sphere of nature is that of necessity. We must choose to accept God's grace; but we must be enabled to make our choice. The basis of the objection, moreover, is a mere speculation. If knowledge of God is always an affair of God's self-revelation, then it will be normally a progressive affair, and there can be no proof that it develops, where there is ignorance of Christ's Revelation, in a mode which requires the special name of "grace".

We are concerned, then, with a knowledge which arises inevitably at some point in a man's life. Is it possible to indicate this point in any way? Can we assume that this knowledge is always available to any sane man? The answer would seem to be that it arises with the appearance of the moral consciousness, but this leads to a number of difficulties which we must postpone for later treatment. For example, what counts as moral consciousness? And what is the precise connection between moral awareness and an awareness of God?

THE "REVOLUTION" IN PHILOSOPHY

Let us now consider the attitudes which Catholics versed in modern philosophy sometimes adopt towards the philosophy of religion. It has been already noted that some of them regard philosophy as fundamentally a matter of logic, but that is only a very general and rough indication of the position. To understand it we must refer very briefly to what has been happening in the philosophical field during the past fifty years. At the beginning of this century philosophy in the English-speaking world was dominated by Hegelianism, the doctrine of an evolving Absolute which is altogether incompatible with belief in the Christian God, although it was often adopted by Protestant and especially Anglican thinkers. F. H. Bradley, not indeed a Hegelian but akin to Hegel in certain respects, offers in his *Appearance and Reality* a dialectic in which the Absolute proves to be an all-embracing Mind of which we ourselves and all the objects of our knowledge are only aspects; in other words, a form of pantheism or panlogism. This is also called idealistic Monism, and it has been pointed out often enough that Karl Marx adopted Hegel's dialectic and also reached a Monistic conclusion; but whereas Hegel said that everything was Mind, Marx said that everything was Matter. Hegelianism makes play with a good many abstractions and metaphysical notions, and Hegelians often used language which does not stand up to the test of a rigorous analysis. That is the remote background of the "revolution in philosophy" as it has been called.

Since the "revolutionary" philosophers are sometimes described as liberating philosophy from Hegelianism, it must be pointed out that Hegelianism was already out of fashion before the "revolution" began. The position was that there was a vacuum waiting to be filled, and the current of thought was already flowing strongly against "metaphysics" (commonly identified with Hegelianism) and "theorizing", against any attempt to build up philosophical systems. The ground was thus prepared for the "revolution". It must not be confused with the Logical Positivism which was in vogue in the 'thirties, and something must first be said about that to emphasize the point. The fundamental principle of Logical Positivism was that we must not go beyond "experience"—we have no right to claim that something exists unless there is the evidence of experience to support our claim. The principle, in this very general form, is surely a sound one. But the Logical Positivists went on to say that the evidence of our senses is the only valid test of truth and that everything which cannot be so tested is meaningless; but this principle is not itself discoverable by sense–experience and that, in the baldest outline, is the reason why Logical Positivism collapsed. The story has often been told, and we are concerned with it here only to distinguish it from the "revolution" itself and to emphasize that the atmosphere in which the "revolution" occurred was an anti-metaphysical atmosphere strongly charged with materialism.

There are, then, no Logical Positivists nowadays. Nobody wishes to connect himself, by accepting that name, with the self-contradictory "verification-principle". It was not until this doctrine had been cleared out of the way that the "revolution" proper began to establish itself. The movement had been gathering strength for some time, and it has no necessary connection with any sort of Positivism (that is, any anti-metaphysical doctrine). It has become known as "Linguistic Analysis" or "Logical Analysis". The earlier "analysts" were, on the whole, anti-metaphysical not because they were analysts but because the general trend of thought for many years past had been anti-metaphysical. Dr M. J. Charlesworth, in his excellent account of the movement, *Philosophy and Linguistic Analysis*,[3] issues the usual warnings against regarding the analysts as a "school", but considers it possible to say that they have a common conception of the nature and purpose of philosophy. "One might say," he writes, "that for the analysts the task of philosophy is to show that philosophical answers or explanations have no meaning, or are irrelevant, because the philosophical questions or problems they are supposed to answer or resolve simply do not arise; and it is the task of Analysis to show that they do not arise when we understand what we are talking about."[4] This must not be taken to mean that all philosophical questions are necessarily meaningless for all analysts but that it is the business of the philosopher to bring this technique to bear upon them. All that can be described as common to the philosophers known as "analysts" is their employment of this technique. Dr Charlesworth points

[3] Duquesne University, Pittsburg, Pa., 1959.
[4] *Op. cit.*, p. 2.

out in his Preface that Linguistic Analysis "has been the dominant influence in English philosophy over the last twenty
years", and that it "has recently begun to have some vogue in
the United States of America". He also points out that it is commonly confused with American Logical Empiricism[5] ("empiricism" may be considered in this connection as the equivalent
of "positivism"). The philosophy of religion need have no
quarrel with this method of analysis in itself. Some philosophical questions may indeed be "dissolved" by it; it is
obviously useful so far as it goes, and it was used, in a less
thoroughgoing way, by philosophers in other ages. Our concern with it is that its practitioners, for the most part, hold all
metaphysical questions at arm's length. Dr Charlesworth com-
ments: "The analysts hold ... that analysis is not connected
necessarily with any particular view of the world or of man's
destiny, and such questions are hardly, if ever, discussed. This
dichotomy between philosophy and 'beliefs' is especially
marked in Wittgenstein's philosophy—it is typical of the movement as a whole and, as such, is undoubtedly one of its greatest
weaknesses."[6]

The "revolution" is not a matter of only local or transient
importance. The influence of Wittgenstein, in particular, is still
growing. The headquarters of the movement, since the war, has
been Oxford, and Oxford philosophy tends to permeate the
English-speaking world. We must expect the effects to be far-
reaching, for a philosophical standpoint once adopted by the
leading philosophers continues to exercise its influence long
after it has been abandoned by its originators or by their successors. In fact, there has been quite recently a certain change
of attitude apparent among English academic philosophers.
It is too soon yet to speak of a definite revival of metaphysics.
But the hostility to metaphysics, after giving place to a sort of
armed neutrality, seems to be turning into a neutrality which,
if not altogether friendly, is at least more open-minded. We
may say that the analysts tend rather to be "unmetaphysical"

[5] *Op. cit.*, p. 5.
[6] *Op. cit.*, p. 8.

than "anti-metaphysical". Nevertheless, the dichotomy between philosophy and "beliefs" remains something to be reckoned with very seriously, and its importance for us at the moment is that it affects Catholics as well as non-Catholics.

CATHOLICS AND THE "REVOLUTION"

This was brought out very clearly in a controversy during the spring and early summer of 1954.[7] A number of Catholic writers, supporters of the "revolution", dissociated themselves altogether from traditional metaphysics and seemed to regard philosophy as a purely neutral science in regard to religion. They were unwilling to discuss proofs of God's existence and could not be brought to state their opinions with any definiteness about the sense of the Vatican Council's pronouncements in the matter.

In the article which summed up the controversy I wrote as follows: "There is a danger that those who have been brought up on linguistic analysis may keep their philosophical views and their religious convictions shut off from one another so that their minds become tinged with an anti-intellectualism which is something like 'fideism'."[8] (A complete disavowal of any philosophy of religion is, as we have seen, opposed to the Church's explicit teaching.)

It will be useful, at this point, to quote from an exceptionally well-informed article by Mr Michael Dummett, a Catholic and an Oxford philosopher. He is criticizing Mr Ernest Gellner's book *Words and Things*, which provoked a long correspondence towards the end of 1959 in *The Times* of London.[9]

I think that most Oxford philosophers ... would not reject the possibility that philosophy could arrive at substantive truths: they would merely say that they do not see how this is to be done, and add that, while much past philosophy makes clear

[7] In the London *Tablet*.
[8] *The Tablet*, June 12th, 1954.
[9] One thing which emerged from this debate was that there is a growing impatience with modern Oxford philosophy.

sense, understood as elucidation of concepts, they have not found a single convincing example of a philosophical demonstration of a substantive truth. I think indeed that a Catholic philosopher would not be content with this position. Natural theology is certainly part of philosophy, and the existence of God is not just a fact about concepts. Nevertheless, I do not see any point in a *general* defence of the view that philosophy can attain substantive truth. What is needed is a convincing philosophical demonstration of some particular substantive truth; whining about philosophers who attempt no such demonstration, without the slightest indication of how this is to be constructed, will not get us anywhere.[10]

There must be a philosophy of religion, Mr Dummett seems to be saying, but I am still waiting for somebody to produce one which is worth looking at, nor do I feel any obligation to do anything about it myself. But it is gratifying to see that he does admit the necessity for some connection between religion and philosophy.

Mr Dummett's words show plainly enough that even a theist philosopher may have a very poor opinion of metaphysics or at least of the present state of metaphysics. And it is of course the general attitude to metaphysics among English philosophers for so many years which is our main concern. The "revolution" is important for our purposes only in relation to this general state of affairs; if it has eased the position in some ways, it has complicated it in others: it encourages the dichotomy between philosophy and "beliefs" by reducing philosophy, in practice, to the elucidating of concepts, to removing misunderstandings, a purely negative business. What we have to say, then, to Catholics who regard philosophy in this way as a matter of logical or linguistic analysis is what we had to say just now to another sort of objector: if you disapprove of the expression "the philosophy of religion" then let us call our field of inquiry by some other name. "Philosophy" can be redefined to suit your requirements, although it would be very odd to do so. All that really matters is that the apprehension

[10] *Blackfriars* (Oxford), March, 1960, p. 78.

of God should be acknowledged as possible, in practice as well as in theory, for the human mind; it follows from this that there is a particular sort of inquiry, call it what you will, which studies the way in which this apprehension occurs and so facilitates its exercise.

THE WIDER CONTEXT

The attitude of typical modern philosophers to the whole question of certainty, of *certain* knowledge, is of such fundamental importance for our purposes that the next chapter must be largely devoted to it. The present chapter will be brought to an end with a few summary conclusions about the general unpopularity of our subject. So far we have dwelt only on those causes of its unpopularity which are immediately relevant to the present undertaking. But we should bear in mind certain related factors. The concentration on biblical studies among our theologians, admirable in itself, has been accompanied by a certain coldness towards metaphysics. The philosophy of religion is not indeed rejected by our "biblical theologians", but it does not receive from them very much encouragement. Among Protestant theologians and philosophers the work of Karl Barth has been for many years the chief deterrent to the pursuit of natural theology, although this has provoked certain admirable reactions from non-Catholic as well as Catholic writers which will be of great use to us in later chapters. And it hardly needs to be said that the reading public at large concerns itself very little with our subject. A revival of interest in religion since the war, in some countries of Western Europe in particular, must not blind us to the indifference to religion which characterizes the great mass of the population in most countries. It may be true that the general indifference of academic philosophers is offset by an increasing respect for religion among leaders of thought in other fields and that this gives us good hope for the distant future; but the influences at present at work give us no ground at all for complacency.

CHAPTER II

OBSTACLES

Before considering any constructive proposals for a philosophy of religion we must take further note of the chief obstacles to any such proposals at the present time. We have seen that there has been a prevailing anti-metaphysical tendency in the world of thought for many years past, but the effects of this tendency have been touched on, so far, only in very general terms. If the problems which it sets us are to be appreciated, we must have before us examples of anti-metaphysical and unmetaphysical productions.

EMPIRICISM AND BELIEF: PROF. BRAITHWAITE

We may usefully begin with a well-known lecture given by Prof. R. B. Braithwaite, who holds a chair of moral philosophy at Cambridge. It is entitled *An Empiricist's View of the Nature of Religious Belief*[1] (an "empiricist" is literally one who takes his stand on "experience", but the word is often, in practice, equivalent with "positivist"). "I will start", Prof. Braithwaite writes, "with the verification principle in the form in which it was originally propounded by logical positivists—that the meaning of any statement is given by its method of verification."[2] Later he points out that "the verification principle of meaning in the hands of empiricist philosophers of the 1930's became modified either by a glossing of the term 'verification' or by a change of the verification principle into the use principle: the meaning of any statement is given by the

[1] Cambridge University Press, 1955.
[2] P. 2.

way in which it is used".[3] This is "no desertion from the spirit
of empiricism", for "the only way of discovering how a statement is used is by an empirical inquiry: a statement need not
be itself empirical, but that it is used in a particular way is
always a straightforwardly empirical proposition". Then "the
kernel for an empiricist of the problem of religious belief is to
explain, in empirical terms, how a religious statement is used
by a man who asserts it in order to express his religious
conviction".[4]

The problem is to see what religious statements *mean*. A
statement "can only be understood by an understanding of the
circumstances which would verify or falsify it". That is, "the
meaning of a religious statement has to be found by discovering the steps which must be taken to ascertain its truth-value".[5]
Prof. Braithwaite refers to "three classes of statement whose
method of truth-value testing is in general outline clear: statements about particular matters of empirical fact, scientific
hypotheses and the logically necessary statements of logic and
mathematics". Religious statements do not fall into any of
these classes. They are not statements about particular empirical facts: "If it is maintained that the *existence* of God is
known by observation, for example, in the self-authenticating
experience of 'meeting God', the term 'God' is being used
merely as a part of this particular experience. Any interesting
theological proposition, e.g. that God is personal, will attribute
a property to God which is not an observable one and so
cannot be known by direct observation".[6] Religious statements are not scientific hypotheses because "if a set of theological propositions are to be regarded as explanations of fact
in the empirical world, they must be refutable by experience.
We must be willing to abandon them if the facts prove to be
different from what we think they are",[7] but philosophers of
religion are not prepared to accept such a condition. Nor do

[3] P. 10.
[4] P. 11.
[5] P. 3.
[6] Pp. 4–5.
[7] P. 6.

religious statements resemble the propositions of logic and mathematics for those propositions "make no assertion of existence".[8] They are laws (if I may summarize Prof. Braithwaite's account very simply) which tell us only that *if* something is the case, *then* something else is also the case.

There is, however, another class of assertions, Prof. Braithwaite continues, moral assertions. He comes to the conclusion that religious assertions must be of this kind. And how are moral assertions used? "According to the view developed by various moral philosophers since the impossibility of regarding moral statements as verifiable propositions was recognized, a moral assertion is used to express the *attitude* of the man making the assertion."[9] He is "subscribing to a policy of action" and "whether or not a man has the intention of pursuing a particular behaviour policy can be empirically tested".[10] Religious assertions, then, are "declarations of commitment to a way of life".[11] The full significance of this conclusion emerges when Prof. Braithwaite writes: "To say that it is belief in the dogmas of religion which is the cause of the believer's intending to behave as he does is to put the cart before the horse; it is the intention to behave which constitutes what is known as religious conviction."[12] If belief in God, instead of causing one to behave in certain ways, is nothing but our intention so to behave, then the philosophy of religion is indeed a dead subject.

But what is a religious policy as distinct from a moral one? Prof. Braithwaite answers that a Christian's assertions that God is love (*agape*) must be taken to "declare his intention to follow an agapeistic way of life".[13] Religions are differentiated by the "stories" to which they are attached, and "it is not necessary for the asserter of a religious assertion to believe in

[8] P. 8.
[9] P. 11.
[10] P. 13.
[11] P. 15.
[12] P. 16.
[13] P. 18.

the truth of the story".[14] Finally, "there is one story common to all the moral theistic religions which has proved of great psychological value in enabling religious men to persevere in carrying out their religious behaviour policies—the story that in so doing they are doing the will of God".[15] God is only a "story".

Prof. Braithwaite's lecture was widely discussed. Many Christian writers, naturally, objected to the reduction of all religious belief to declarations of "behaviour policies" and "stories". But it cannot be said that much was done to put up a philosophical case in reply to this dismissal of the traditional arguments for God's existence. Four articles appeared in *The Cambridge Review* in 1956. Mr F. N. Schofield argued that God's existence is a hypothesis which is sufficiently attested by "Christian experience". Prof. D. M. Mackinnon, on the other hand, agreed with Prof. Braithwaite in rejecting a "self-authenticating experience" and went on to emphasize the difficulties which anyone familiar with modern philosophy must feel about the notions of cause and substance when "ontological divinity" is in debate and about "the most subtle and perplexing logic" of the word "creative". Only Prof. Ramsey, of Oxford, made any attempt to offer evidence for God's existence by describing certain circumstances in which the word "God" is posited and given an empirical anchorage. "It does not follow", he pointed out, "that the only alternative to 'straightforwardly empirical' is 'fictional'." Prof. Braithwaite, summing up in the fourth article, remarked that "a characterization of Christian belief in terms of knowledge of some inexplicable way of thinking will only save an 'intellectual content' for Christianity at the price of making it a secret doctrine open only to the Elect". But it seems clear that if men have a knowledge of God it cannot be "empirical" in the anti-metaphysical sense in which Prof. Braithwaite and so many modern philosophers use the term. It may also be becoming clear that such knowledge must be in

[14] Pp. 25–6.
[15] Pp. 30–1.

some sense empirical if it is to be considered seriously by our
academic philosophers.

THE MODERN DISLIKE OF METAPHYSICS: TWO RECENT SYMPOSIA

Anyone who wishes to satisfy himself more fully on these
points has only to look at *New Essays in Philosophical Theology*, edited by Prof. Antony Flew and Mr Alastair McIntyre
and published by the Student Christian Movement in 1955.
The editors tell us that the Christian and the non-Christian
contributors are divided "just about equally". The uninitiated
reader would not find it easy to decide which were which, and
the Christian editor, Mr McIntyre, confines himself in his own
contribution to showing that "visions" do not provide valid
ground for religious belief. This would be all right if valid
ground were provided elsewhere in the book, but with one
exception (to be noted presently) none of the contributors
makes any serious attempt to do this. (We are told in the
Preface that what they have in common is a "familiarity with
and a general indebtedness to the recent revolution in philosophy".) The purpose of Prof. J. J. C. Smart's paper, on "The
existence of God", is "not to discuss whether God exists" but
"to discuss certain arguments". After a good deal of destructive
criticism, Prof. Smart concludes that he wants to go on asking
the question: why should anything exist at all?—"although
logic seems to tell us that the only answer which is not absurd
is to say 'why shouldn't it?' ". That might have proved a starting-point for a useful inquiry, but nothing comes of it. Other
contributors take the same "empiricist" line as Prof. Braithwaite and seem to think, as he does, that metaphysics has been
ruled out when the only necessary propositions are found to be
those of logic and mathematics: here we may point out that
when a metaphysician says "God is necessary" he is referring,
not to logical necessity, but to the sovereign independence, the
absoluteness, of God.

Both Prof. Flew and Prof. Smart, in discussing the problem

of evil, reject the appeal to free will as a partial solution on
the ground that it is not contradictory to say that God could
have so made us that we should always freely choose the right.
This introduces us to a fresh aspect of the present philosophical
position to which we shall return: the rejection of free moral
choice in the sense in which Christians understand it. "Freedom" is understood, by these philosophers, as a willingness or
a mere lack of constraint, and the element of responsibility
is eliminated. To say that we could have chosen otherwise does
not mean, for them, that we had it in our power at the moment
of choice to do right or wrong but merely that we should have
chosen otherwise if circumstances had been other than they
were. A Christian must say that this is not what he means by
choice. But this must be discussed more fully later.

The only paper in *New Essays in Philosophical Theology*
which makes any serious attempt to be constructive is that by
Mr I. M. Crombie. He points out that "theistic interpretations
...cannot be assessed by asking whether they conform to the
laws of logic or of scientific method... in stating them we find
ourselves saying things which we cannot literally mean...the
sense of dependence feels not at all like being persuaded by
arguments but like seeing...". When he goes on to say that
unless there were "concrete events which we felt impelled to
interpret as divine we could not know that the notion of divinity
had any application to reality", he seems to be saying that we
can have no genuine knowledge of God without Revelation.
Nevertheless, he writes that "there must exist within a man's
mind the contrast between the contingent and the necessary, the
derivative and the underivative, the finite and the infinite, the
perfect and the imperfect, if anything is to be for him a revelation of God". Again we see that in so far as any positive proposals are brought forward, they are based on some sort of
"empiricism". The general impression left by the book is that
theists are in a pretty hopeless position nowadays and that their
attempts to extricate themselves are very feeble indeed.

Faith and Logic (Oxford Essays in Philosophical Theology)
appeared in 1956. The title suggests that it is a reply to the

volume which we have been considering, but this is hardly
the case. None of the contributors says anything at all definite
about the central metaphysical issue, the question of God's
existence. Mr J. R. Lucas' paper on the soul is, however, of
great value and most relevant to the purpose of this chapter.
One of the results of "empiricism" which is obviously of first-
class importance for the philosopher of religion is the doubt
which many "empiricists" feel about the existence of a con-
tinuous "self". When this self is called the "soul" they are still
more shy of it. The existence of the soul is a highly problemati-
cal affair for the philosophers of the "revolution"; even those
of them who are Catholics are often very unwilling to commit
themselves about it as philosophers. Mr Lucas deals with this
in an admirably forthright way. Belief in the soul, he writes,
means that "Persons can be the subject of a discourse in which
there are predicated of them attributes and qualities which cannot be properly predicated about things". The following passage will give a good idea of the way in which philosophers
have been reducing the soul to a "thing":

> Our final reason for repudiating the reductive analysis of
> mind and spirit to patterns of behaviour is our own first-personal
> experience. Exception may be taken to the language of intro-
> spection and privileged access in so far as these metaphors sug-
> gest an inward eye peculiarly well placed for seeing through an
> internal aperture to an internal screen beyond. But that each
> person is not in a privileged position for self-knowledge, that
> when we have twinges of pain they are not "mental occurrences"
> but, basically, dispositions to give certain sorts of answer to
> doctor's questions—to this doctrine if seriously maintained, we
> can only reply, with St Augustine, *Da veniam, non credimus.*[16]

(We shall have more to say shortly about this doctrine of
"dispositions".)

Mr Lucas takes as his chief example of the reductive analysis
of the soul *The Concept of Mind*, by Gilbert Ryle, Professor
of Philosophy in Oxford and the Editor of *Mind*. Here an
illustration of Prof. Ryle's method may be given from a later

[16] "I'm sorry, but I don't believe you."

book, *Dilemmas*.[17] He is discussing the meaning of the word "seeing". "Seeing", he tells us, "does not refer to a power or a state at all. I can be looking for or looking at something, but I cannot be seeing it. At any given moment I have not yet seen it or I have now seen it. The verb 'to see' does not signify an experience, i.e. something I go through, am engaged in. It does not signify a sub-stretch of my life-story."[18] What, then, does it signify? In the only passage which suggests an answer Prof. Ryle's compares "seeing" with "winning": "Where winning is the scoring of an athletic success, perceiving is the scoring of a investigational success."[19]

THE ATTACK UPON THE INTELLECT: THE INFLUENCE OF PROF. RYLE

What Prof. Ryle is anxious to avoid is the conclusion that "seeing" is an introspective "mental occurrence". It looks as though our own intellective awareness is now in doubt. And we shall soon see that this is indeed the situation with which we are faced. If everything is reduced to sense-experience and the rules of logic, *intellection*, knowledge of the *truth*, seems to have no place. We may see how such a conclusion can be reached by a philosopher who accepts Prof. Ryle's general position if we turn to Mr John Hartland-Swann's book *An Analysis of Knowing*.[20] We shall find ourselves faced with the most fundamental of all obstacles to the philosopher of religion, the rejection of *certainty* altogether.

Mr Hartland-Swann considers that "the great analytical task" performed in *The Concept of Mind* "does not go far enough" (p. 10). (Prof. Ryle has read his proofs, we are told in the Prefatory Notes, and has made "many valuable suggestions and criticisms from which I hope to have profited".)[21] In

[17] Cambridge University Press, 1954.
[18] P. 103.
[19] *Ibid*.
[20] Allen and Unwin, 1958.
[21] The substance of the paragraph which follows is taken from my notice in *The Tablet* of July 19th, 1958.

his introductory chapter Mr Hartland-Swann warns us against
the concept of "being directly aware of" when we are talking
about "knowing". In his second chapter he informs us that
when we say we know something to be the case what we really
mean is that we have decided or accepted a decision that it is
the case. Of course many sentences with "know" in them can
be rephrased so as to fit Mr Hartland-Swann's requirements,
and a considerable part of the book is taken up with analysis
of this kind. The difference between correct and incorrect
decisions is, according to Mr Hartland-Swann, that the former
are generally accepted (these he calls "dominant decisions")
and the latter not. But

> a dominant decision . . . can always be disputed; and if it can
> be successfully disputed—if, that is, it can be made to appear
> to a large enough, or influential enough, body of people as no
> longer appropriate to the evidence—then it will be generally
> abandoned. When, therefore, we say that a dominant decision
> has been found to be incorrect, we imply, by our use of the word
> "incorrect", that the original decision has been superseded and
> is no longer in harmony with what is or will be the new domi-
> nant decision.[22]

It seems rather obvious that the question now arises: how
do we decide that a decision once arrived at is no longer
appropriate to the evidence? Is it because so many other people
have already decided this? If so, how have they decided it?
There's a hole in my bucket, dear Liza. . . . It begins to look,
after all, as though at some stage *somebody* has really to *know*
something, even in Mr Hartland-Swann's account of the matter.
He does later admit that we "notice" things. But, as we shall
see more fully later, there is nothing nasty and metaphysical
about that, for "noticing" can never be "indubitable". We may
be said to "come across" things, in other words, but we can
never be *certain* that we are doing so in any case—so that the
admission provides little comfort for the philosopher of
religion.

[22] P. 22.

In his third chapter Mr Hartland-Swann concludes that it is justifiable to say "I know" if my decision is "well-grounded", but since that proves to mean only "in accordance with the dominant decision of those generally regarded as experts" or "the dominant decision of people regarded as normal and intelligent", it gets us no further. When there are no dominant decisions available, "the modern philosopher", we are told, "can be of help in sorting out the issues involved . . . today the question 'Does God exist?' invites, from a philosopher, neither a 'know' nor a 'believe' statement; it invites an analysis of 'God' and 'exists' ".[23] The passage is characteristic of analyst writers. It is indeed true that we must ask ourselves what we mean by "God"; but we did not have to wait for the logical analysts to tell us this. And it is not the only question which can demand (and receive) an answer in this connection, unless we take up with Mr Hartland-Swann's "reduction" of knowledge.

He goes on to say that "we cannot 'get at' facts except metaphorically; we can only decide that they are so and so. When such decisions become dominant they license some statements, thereby making them 'correct', and veto other statements, thereby making them 'incorrect'; but we have at the same time to remember that there is nothing sacrosanct about any dominant decision. . . ."[24] (It is difficult to understand how Mr Hartland-Swann can claim on the following page that he has conducted his analysis "without playing into the hands of the sceptics".) The point is brought out all too clearly in the following passage:

> Once . . . we realize that those who claim to know that promise-keeping, truth-telling, self-improvement and so forth are duties are merely expressing decisions (which they think ought to be dominant decisions), we cease to worry whether it is philosophically justifiable or not to use "know" in this context; and we turn our attention to the more profitable task of

[23] Pp. 43–4.
[24] P. 47.

analysing the logical behaviour of ethical concepts and the judgements in which they are embedded.[25]

It seems useless to suggest to Mr Hartland-Swann that morality is more than a matter of personal preferences, because he would presumably reply that we are only recommending that there should be a dominant decision to this effect.

The fourth chapter seeks to show that "all cases of knowing *that* can be ultimately reduced to cases of knowing *how*", which leads to the following remarkable assertion: "When you query whether my tooth is being drilled, I am able to reply correctly that it is—and this is what I mean by saying that I know that my tooth is now being drilled.... I am able (know how) to reply correctly."[26] This is the reduction of knowledge to a "disposition" which we encountered earlier in this chapter. Mr Hartland-Swann is not overlooking the sensation of having one's tooth drilled. His view is that, "although know-claims are usually based on occurrences", knowing *that* something is the case does not report any occurrence—it implies a capacity. We naturally ask, at this point, whether we are not simply aware of "occurrences" and why this awareness is not to be called "knowledge". Mr Hartland-Swann, as we have seen, deprecates talk about "awareness". He refers at one point to the "mystical relation often supposed to hold between myself and my sense-data".[27] Well, not mystical, but still surely highly mysterious, unanalysable—in fact, metaphysical. No, says Mr. Hartland-Swann, you may speak of being "directly aware" if you really want to, but only if it is recognized that this expression carries no esoteric connotation of "indubitable knowing" along with its obvious connotation of one form of noticing.[28] He rejects

the assumption that knowing and believing are mental acts— acts which are, of course, directed towards some object ... all we need, in order to put ourselves on the right track at the

[25] P. 52.
[26] P. 61.
[27] P. 67.
[28] P. 92.

outset is to grasp, what is now generally accepted, that "believing" is a purely dispositional verb. Hence when I say that Jones believes something, I am not referring to any mental act which is supposed to be going on in Jones's head, I am merely telling you that, given the appropriate circumstances, Jones is disposed to *react* in certain ways.[29]

Finally we read: "My so-called direct knowledge of my experience turns out to be simply my capacity to make correct statements *about* my experience, or to the effect *that* my experiences are such and such. There is nothing mysteriously direct about my *knowing*; it is merely that the evidential basis of my know-claim is my own private experience."[30] And since such experiences do not give us, according to Mr Hartland-Swann, any indubitable information about anything, the notion of *truth* cannot be saved by appealing to them. It has been entirely evacuated.

PROF. AYER ON CERTAINTY: MR JOHN WILSON ON FREE WILL

To complete the gloomy picture which this chapter has been painting a few short excerpts will be given from two recent books of peculiar interest. The first is *The Problem of Knowledge*[31] by A. J. Ayer, now Professor of Logic at Oxford. Prof. Ayer is perhaps better known to the general public than any other contemporary English philosopher except Lord Russell. In this book he purports to meet "sceptical arguments". But in fact he provides us with particularly clear examples of that rejection of absolute certainty which is so regular a feature of philosophical writing in our time. He remarks that "from the fact that someone is convinced that something is true, however firm his conviction may be, it never follows logically that it is true.... It must always remains possible that one is mistaken".[32] Obviously we *can* always make mistakes by making

[29] P. 96.
[30] P. 134.
[31] Pelican Edition, 1950.
[32] Pp. 19 and 22.

judgements which go beyond our evidence. The question is: can we ever be sure of avoiding mistakes by confining ourselves to what is strictly evidence? If we cannot, if there is no such thing as sheer indubitable evidence, then we are in a hopeless position—there is no firm ground to build on; we never know where we are. And Prof. Ayer does not allow us to say that we are certain of our own experiences: "Experiences themselves are neither certain nor uncertain; they simply occur."[33] So he is concerned not with experiences but with statements. He does at once point admit that the statement "I feel a headache" is "perfectly assured" in so far as "there is nothing for one to be uncertain or mistaken about".[34] But this is not *knowledge*, and his general conclusion is that, although "there are a great many statements the truth of which we rightly do not doubt", yet "the philosopher's ideal of certainty has no application".[35] It is not at all clear why we are right not to doubt these statements, if we cannot rely at any time on our own certainty, for, as we shall see later, there is nothing else in the long run on which we can rely. The sceptical arguments, then, have *not* been met.

We must also notice what Prof. Ayer has to say about the knowledge of one's own existence. Descartes' famous formula "I think, therefore I am" only proves, he tells us, that *if* a man thinks, he must exist—it does not prove that any one *in fact* knows anything: "It simply makes the logical point that one sort of statement follows from another . . . this does not show that these statements are in any way sacrosanct, considered in themselves."[36] But can one not be infallibly certain that one is in fact doubting here and now? Apparently not. Moreover, "the consciousness of one's self is not an experience among others, not even, as some have thought, a special experience which accompanies all the others".[37]

Finally let us note Mr John Wilson's view of moral choice

[33] P. 52.
[34] P. 56.
[35] P. 68.
[36] Pp. 46–7.
[37] P. 48.

in his book *Language and Christian Belief*.[38] The publishers tell us that "he teaches divinity in the Sixth Form of a public school" and "seeks to bridge the gulf between faith and reason". Like Prof. Flew and others, he rejects the "free will defence" in regard to the problem of evil. Freedom, he writes, "necessitates only the absence of compulsion. . . . When it is the man himself, and not something outside him which chooses, we say that he is free". But our choices are only "the result of anterior states of merit, character, motives, etc."; they are not "in principle unpredictable".[39] This clearly excludes moral choice in the sense of choosing evil when we had it in our power to choose good. It seems, then, that the most significant facts of the moral life are also rejected by contemporary philosophers, even by those who call themselves Christians. Is there any hope left for a philosophy of religion?

[38] Macmillan, 1959.
[39] P. 72.

CHAPTER III

CLEARING THE GROUND

In the last chapter it became clear that modern "empiricists" do not allow us to appeal to anything beyond experience and the laws of logic, and at the same time do not grant immunity from error to any of our experiences. Moreover, their notion of "experience" is, I shall suggest, a constricted one. It seemed proper, therefore, to call them "empiricists" in inverted commas.

EXPERIENCE AS SELF-GUARANTEEING

Clearly we must find a more solid basis if we are to show how a philosophy of religion can be built up. And we shall find material for this easily enough if we examine some of the admissions which Prof. Ayer, like all honest sceptics, is compelled to make in the book which we have just been discussing. But before doing this it will be useful to take another look at Mr Wilson's book, for it contains passages which a philosopher of religion must consider very seriously: it is time to point out that we have been concentrating so far only on the more deplorable views of the "empiricists" and that they have other things to say to us which are at least less obviously contrary to the dictates of the Christian conscience or to commonsense. In his first chapter Mr Wilson discusses the familiar doctrine that God "transcends" human experience. He remarks:

> Either "God" stands for some thing at least partly within our experience, so that statements with the word "God" in them are to that extent experimentally verifiable; or else "God" does not

stand for something within our actual or potential experience,
in which case (to put it bluntly) statements about God can have
no possible interest for us, and may well be meaningless ... if
a descriptive word is supposed to refer to something which
could not be experienced, then it seems doubtful whether it
describes anything at all.[1]

This puts before us very forcibly the difficulty of getting
"beyond" experience. Obviously we have to start with experience. Shall we have to remain within it, in some sense, throughout our inquiry? Mr Wilson remarks later that believers must
"lay down some sort of agreed tests for their assertions, by
means of religious experience", if they "expect anyone to place
rational belief in them".[2] Shall we be able to avoid an appeal
to "religious experience" in some sense of that much-abused
expression if we are to give any meaning to religious assertions? This may suggest that the topic on which we shall now
embark, that of our fundamental certainties or basic experiences, is not just a necessary preliminary but something which
we shall have to keep before our minds at all stages.

Let us now return to Prof. Ayer. The reader will have won-
dered, perhaps, how Prof. Ayer succeeds in dodging the conclusion that the experience must be our ultimate guarantee,
if indeed we have one. To examine his attempts to do so will
be a good way of satisfying ourselves that we are in fact
absolutely certain of some things. Are we not absolutely certain, for example, that *if* whales are mammals and if all
mammals breathe through their lungs, *then* whales breathe
through their lungs? Can we succeed in casting the faintest
shadow of doubt on the fact that the conclusion follows from
the premises? Can we suppose that anything could transpire
which would show us to be in error here? Once we have put
the premises together and *seen* the conclusion emerge from
them, there can be no going back. Prof. Ayer seems to be giving
us all that we require when he writes: "We do just have to see
that certain proofs are valid, and it is through having some

[1] P. 10.
[2] P. 31.

experience that we discover the truth or falsity of any empirical fact." But he adds that "what verifies the statement is the existence of the experience, not the confidence that we may have in some description of it".[3] "Feeling certain", that is to say, is not to the point. Now if by "feeling certain" we mean only "having no doubt" it is certainly not to the point. For we can often have no doubt about something and yet prove to be wrong. Nor is "feeling" to the point, if what we are talking about is "only a feeling". But when we say that we "feel certain" that the conclusion about the breathing of whales *is* a conclusion, that it *does* follow, we mean that we *see* it and that we also see that there can be no sort of question about it. To this extent we are infallible. We have a certain experience, an intellective experience of certainty. To the ultimate question: how can you be sure that you are seeing it? we can only reply "I just *am* sure". The experience and the confidence which we have in it are all one thing. Prof. Ayer treats them as separate and in doing so rejects the intellective character of our certainty. And this leads us to the all-important conclusion, which should be quite obvious, that all experience, precisely as such, is certain experience.

METAPHYSICS AND COMMONSENSE: PROF. AYER AGAIN

Let us take an example of this from Prof. Ayer's book. He considers, as we saw earlier, "feeling a headache". He points out that one might feel a headache, record the fact in a diary and then come to doubt the veracity of the record. The sentence "I feel a headache now" and "I didn't feel a headache then" are, he says, contradictory versions of the same "state of affairs".[4] But there are two "states of affairs". In the first I *know* that I have a headache; in the second I forget whether I had a headache or not. Prof. Ayer accuses those who accept absolute certainty of describing the state of affairs in terms

[3] P. 21.
[4] P. 55.

only of the knowing subject. He himself describes it in terms only of the known object. But certainty, which is our fundamental cognitive experience, is precisely the meeting of subject and object. The headache is directly present to my consciousness. In so far as I "register" this I cannot make a mistake. It is only when I go beyond my immediate evidence that I can go wrong. (Nor does it seem necessary for me to frame a sentence in order to distinguish feeling a pain in the head from not feeling one.) "We are dissociating having an experience", writes Prof. Ayer, "from knowing that one has it."[5] But this is surely a very odd thing to do. For to experience something is to know that is it there.

Prof. Ayer writes that "to be in a position to say" that a statement is valid "we must be able to see that it is so, but it is not made valid by our seeing that it is".[6] The statement is indeed valid before we see it, but our seeing it, let me repeat, is *our* guarantee that it is valid. But Prof. Ayer is not interested in the question of *our* guarantee. He continues to harp on the fact that it is the objective state of affairs which makes anything true (as of course it is) and fails to face the question: how can *you* be sure that you really *know* it? He claims to refute the mistaken doctrine that knowing is an infallible state of mind—as if the defenders of the doctrine supposed that it was *only* a state of mind and not also an awareness of an object.[7] It is, in fact, an *intellectual* experience.

The root of the trouble seems to be an unwillingness to take any interest in a conclusion unless it follows logically from something else. Prof. Ayer is always insisting that the truth of a conclusion cannot follow logically from our conviction of it. But there is no need for it to do so. When we in fact *see* something, no question of proof arises. "Seeing" *is* the

[5] P. 67.
[6] P. 22.
[7] When this chapter had been written a very gratifying confirmation of the doctrine of certainty in general was afforded by Prof. C. A. Campbell's article "Self-Evidence" in *The Philosophical Quarterly* for April, 1960. Cf. also the excellent first chapter in Dr Hawkins' *Man and Morals* (Sheed and Ward, 1960).

proof. Certainty is a *fact*, not a question to be decided by logic. And the reason, I think, why Prof. Ayer will not accept this is that our fundamental experience cannot be described in straightforwardly "empirical" terms, precisely because it is the basis of all our mental operations. Thus he complains that philosophers who assert

> some infallible state of consciousness [are] led into difficulties which might have been avoided . . . they have perplexed themselves with such questions as what consciousness is in itself and how it is related to the things, or facts, which are its objects. It does not seem to be identified with its objects, yet neither does it seem to be anything apart from them. . . . When there is added the further premise that consciousness is also self-consciousness, the problem becomes more complicated still.[8]

But it will not do to brush such questions aside because they are not amenable to logical or scientific treatment. They are real questions. We cannot help using the sort of language about knowledge which Prof. Ayer deplores. It may seem very queer that the mind should be its own object: perhaps this is not the most suitable way of describing self-consciousness, but in any case it is difficult to avoid saying something peculiar about it because it is a peculiar affair, in the sense of being unlike anything else. But there is no reason why there should not be things which are peculiar in this sense. Self-consciousness cannot be isolated from consciousness of other things and other persons, and that makes it hard to describe. We cannot point to it by showing what difference it makes to our experience— there are no situations in our experience which lack it to be compared with those which contain it. But it is obviously there, and we know what it is without having to describe it, even to ourselves: it is something of which we are certain—unless modern philosophy has robbed us of our certainty by confusing our minds. Once we have adopted a genuinely empirical method, an unprejudiced one, it should not take us long to realize that the continuity of the self is also something of which

8 P. 23.

we are certain. This too is peculiar—not only in the sense that it is unlike anything else but also in the sense that our knowledge of the continuing self is a very obscure knowledge. Perhaps some people fail to acquire it. I can only ask the reader to think about it. If he fails to acquire it there is nothing in particular to be done about it. Something, I should be obliged to say, is radically wrong with him, and every case would require its own special treatment. For truth is one and error manifold.

The obstacles which we encountered in the last chapter must all be surmounted in the same way. Personal responsibility is something of which we are certain—or can be certain—by the same token. The "empiricists" are casting doubt on facts—facts of experience. These are not matters for argument or for logical techniques. Metaphysics begins in commonsense.

The fact of knowledge is the central one. As soon as we admit that we can know anything as it is a metaphysical prospect opens out before us. It would be more comfortable if we could lock ourselves up in a room of our own with only the laws of logic and our sense-experiences to keep us safe and warm. But draughts from the outer world interfere. The laws of logic are not our private property, and the world on which our experiences depend is a public one. We may be certain that there are other bodies in the world besides our own, and other people. But it is the public character of truth that is the most explosive of our discoveries. To be certain of something does not mean just that for some inscrutable reason I am unable to think of it otherwise than I do. It means that everybody else ought to think of it as I do. (Again, if anybody doesn't accept that, there is no way of *proving* it to him by logical steps—because it is *basic*.) As we have seen, if I follow a piece of reasoning (whales are mammals, all mammals breathe through lungs, therefore . . .), I am certain of the fact that, if these things are so, the conclusion *follows*, and if anybody denies that it does I should have no hesitation in putting him down as a fool. Truth is an absolute standard which all minds must obey. That my limited mind should thus have

access to an absolute standard is the most disturbing thing
of all. I am not identical with it (to use the language
which Prof. Ayer so much dislikes), but I am nothing of
a man apart from it.

THE QUESTION OF SYLLOGISTIC INFERENCE:
M. MARITAIN

But we shall not advance further, at present, along those
lines. For a question arises at this point which must be considered at once. It is a question of method, and it will engage
us for some time. Now that we have claimed certain knowledge
of observable facts, can we not proceed on this basis to prove
God's existence simply by a process of reasoning, that is, by a
movement of thought like that which showed us how the whale
breathes? Can we not prove that God exists as something which
follows from acknowledged facts? Can we not put two
premisses together and produce God's existence as the conclusion? Isn't it, to use the technical term, an affair of "syllogistic inference"?

We must first make it clear that those who maintain that it
is such an affair do not claim that we can start from any fact
of experience and then demonstrate that God exists without
more ado and in a foolproof way; they tell us that we require
also certain philosophical *principles*. M. Maritain, for example, tells us that in order to "grasp on the level of critical
reflection the demonstrative value of the philosophical proofs
of God's existence" one ought to know (among other things)
"that the being of things is not one and the same in all things,
but differs in each, while being grasped by the same idea of
Being and expressed by the same word (this is what Thomists
call the analogy of being . . .) . . . that the laws of being have as
broad an extension as being itself" and that this applies in
particular to the "principle of causality".[9] This may seem a tall
order. But I mention these doctrines at the moment, not to
discuss their difficulties, but simply to avoid misrepresenting

[9] *Approaches to God*, Allen and Unwin, 1955, pp. 16–17.

those who regard the Thomist arguments for God's existence—
St Thomas' "Five Ways"—as syllogisms which provide us,
eventually, with our answer. The point is that they will not do
so, according to these philosophers, unless we bring to bear on
them a certain understanding of Thomist metaphysics. And it
must be added that many modern Thomists, including M. Maritain, admit that there is a "natural pre-philosophical awareness" of God which "involves a reasoning after the fashion of
an intuitive grasp, bathed in the primordial intuition of
existence".[10] We shall discuss this attempt to combine an "intuitive" element with syllogistic reasoning in the next chapter.

We can, however, satisfy ourselves, so it seems to me, on
the question of method without involving ourselves in Thomist
metaphysics. Let us consider in more detail how the whale-
syllogism works out. If all mammals belong to the "breath-
ing-through-lungs" class and if the whale belongs to the class
of mammals, then whales belong to the "breathing-through-
lungs" class. If point A is within circle B and circle B is within
circle C, then A falls within C. It should be clear that this sort
of reasoning cannot produce *God* as its conclusion—however
much it may be "bathed in the primordial intuition of existence" (whatever that may be)—because God is not a member
of any class. Nobody has yet produced for me a syllogism with
premisses which are acceptable to an agnostic and from which
the conclusion "God exists" follows. A syllogism starting with
"if contingent beings exist, then God exists" and going on with
"but contingent beings do exist" seems quite unhelpful. In the
first premiss we ask someone to admit that God's existence is
implied by the world around us, which is just what we are
supposed to be demonstrating.

Either we are using "contingent" in a way which presupposes
the desired answer or else it will be no good to us. The real state
of affairs is that the person to whom we are talking doesn't see
that the world is a *dependent* one. How is he to be brought to
see this? The syllogism is useful for organizing our experiences,
for reaching conclusions which are on the same level as the

[10] *Op. cit.*, p. 8.

experiences on which they depend. But what we need here is not a horizontal movement, but a vertical one. We have to exhibit a new dimension.

It seems to me, then, perfectly clear that the transition from finite to infinite cannot be effected by this sort of inferential process, and the upholders of inference do not offer us any other sort. Whatever the value of Thomist metaphysics may be, if it is supposed to issue in an inferential process as the final stage of the argument, then the argument cannot work. And it must now be pointed out that the introduction of "analogy" into the picture only produces further difficulties. Fr Garrigou-Lagrange, for example, in *God, His Existence and Nature*,[11] which is regularly referred to as the standard work on the subject,[12] offers us the following syllogism: *The world necessarily depends on an extrinsic first cause. Now we call the extrinsic first cause by the name of God. Therefore God exists.*[13] As before, no agnostic will accept the first premiss, because it contains the conclusion. But there is the further difficulty that the word "cause" is said to be "analogous"—that is, our concept of cause is applicable to God as well as to creatures. If it is not being applied to God in the first premiss, then it cannot be applied to him in the conclusion, because in that case nothing would follow.

The following is the general argument which, Fr Garrigou-Lagrange concludes, sums up all St Thomas' proofs: "that which does not exist by itself can exist only by another which is self-evident. Now there are beings ... which do not exist of and by themselves. *Ergo.*"[14] Again if the principle of causality laid down in the first of these statements does not already include *God's* causality, then *God's* causality cannot be found in the conclusion. There is, then, no need for us to examine the "Five Ways" in detail in the present connection. As M. Maritain notes at one point,[15] "the nerve of the proof, the formal

[11] St Louis, Herder, 1934.
[12] As in the Preface to M. Maritain's *Approaches to God.*
[13] Pp. 224–5.
[14] P. 381.
[15] *Op. cit.*, p. 8.

principle of the demonstration, is the same in each of the five ways, to wit, the necessity of a first cause which is pure Act or Being, itself subsistent in its own right". It should be clear that this principle on which all depends cannot be itself demonstrated syllogistically, and that the acceptance of it is in effect the acceptance of the required conclusion. It is, of course, possible to erect a syllogism on the basis of it, and that is what Fr Garrigou-Lagrange has done in the passage quoted in the last paragraph. It is a valid syllogism, but it does not prove that God exists. It proves *for anyone who admits an infinite first cause* that what theists call "God" exists. But the point at issue is whether there *is* an infinite first cause. Finally, we may note that the question of God's existence could not depend upon drawing a conclusion from the premisses of a syllogism for the further reason that nobody in his senses can fail to draw such a conclusion. Whatever it is that prevents intelligent people from admitting God's existence, it cannot be the inability to syllogize. The root of the difficulty, on any showing, must lie elsewhere.

It must be emphasized that there is no question here of dismissing the Thomist "proofs" as invalid and useless except in so far as they claim to be syllogisms beginning on neutral ground—on ground which the agnostic may be expected to acknowledge—and concluding by force of inference to the existence of God. Nor is it suggested that St Thomas himself regarded the "Ways" in this light. Here I may quote the words of Fr Victor White, O.P. The "Ways" are, he tells us, "in fact and intention, much more the embodiment of our apprehensions in a form of discourse than the question-begging syllogistic concoctions ...".[16] Nevertheless, Thomists continue to maintain that an inferential process is required, and I cannot discover what this could be if it is not a syllogistic process.

[16] *The Downside Review*, 1958, p. 42.

THE THOMIST INSISTENCE ON INFERENCE:
DR HAWKINS

It is suggested, however, by Thomist writers that there is such a thing as a "natural" or "informal" inference. Such a statement as "the world must have a cause" (which sums up the sort of process which they have in mind) is not, as it stands, an inference at all. It is a claim—and one which is simply rejected by non-theists, who may accept causality in the scientific field, causality *in* the world, but cannot be brought from this position by any logical means to accept a metaphysical cause, a cause *of* the world. If "the world must have a cause" proves to *imply* an inference, then the (supposed) probative form of the statement must lie in the inferential process itself which is present in an unformulated way. It must be made explicit, and we are then back where we were. But usually Thomists refer to "informal" inference only to rebut the charge that they make the discovery of God too technical an affair. Indeed, upon inspection, it proves to be so untechnical that it does not look like an inference at all. The Catholic faithful, in so far as they discuss such things, commonly call it an inference because most of them are unaccustomed to philosophical distinctions and are content to accept the common view. What they really mean by "the world must have a cause" is, perhaps, that it is irrational to deny the world's dependence upon God, if you know that God exists. They are not really considering how anyone comes to know anything of God in the first place.

The chief reason for the Thomist insistence on inference in this connection seems to be the supposition that the only alternative to an inferential process is an immediate vision of God. I shall be contesting this supposition in later chapters. Dr Hawkins, for example, writing in *The New Outline of Modern Knowledge*,[17] after an admirably fair-minded account of the objections to the Thomist inferential proofs (urged by so many philosophers of various persuasions) remarks that "it is scarcely

[17] Ed. A. Pryce-Jones, Gollancz, 1956.

possible to doubt that knowledge must be either immediate or mediate, i.e. inferential".[18] He goes on to defend the inferential proofs by the usual appeal to analogy:

> We know being as what is common to all things. . . . In reasoning about God we use the completely analogous concept of being and some other highly analogous concepts. Causation appears in experience in various forms . . . the recognition that being which is caused in any way presupposes totally uncaused being is followed, in virtue of the analogy or elasticity of being, by the recognition that uncaused necessary being can only be the infinite fullness of being. . . . The Thomist, then, holds that the use of analogous concepts does not vitiate his reasoning. There is sufficient community of meaning in their different modes of instantiation to make valid inference possible.[19]

I have chosen the passages from Dr Hawkins' account which seem most relevant to the present discussion, but it will be seen that none of them contains a syllogism which claims to demonstrate God's existence. Nor can we gather from any of them how such an argument could be constructed. We can see, perhaps, how an argument could be constructed to show, once the analogous concept of being has been accepted *and once the existence of totally uncaused being has been recognized,* that "totally uncaused being" is what men call God. But what we still want to know is how the existence of "totally uncaused being" is made known to us; all we are told is that there is a "recognition that being which is caused in any way presupposes totally uncaused being". Is this recognition operated by a syllogism? And the "analogous concept of being" leads to further difficulties. If this concept refers both to God and to creatures, then the acceptance of such a concept will be equivalent to the acceptance of God's existence, and syllogistic inference will be again ruled out. But there is also the suggestion that there is common ground between the finite and Infinite in the reference to a "sufficient community of meaning". It is important to take our stand at once about this. Once the existence

[18] P. 56.
[19] Pp. 58-9.

of God has been recognized, we are entitled to say that creatures are "likenesses" or "reflections" of God because they prove to stand in a certain metaphysical relation to him of a unique kind (which can be pointed to only by the use of such metaphors). But there should be no question of claiming common ground at any stage, and we certainly cannot appeal to "analogy" as providing such common ground and then use it as a means of *logical transition* from finite to Infinite. This conclusion was reached by the Thomist writer Penido in the well-known statement: "Analogy begins where the Five Ways end." [20]

FR C. B. DALY ON "THE KNOWABLENESS OF GOD"

The latest attempt, at the time of writing, to offer a satisfactory Thomist account of "The Knowableness of God" is a massive article with that title by Fr C. B. Daly.[21] The author is especially concerned with "analysts" and "existentialists" and gives a fully-documented presentation of the present position which is in many ways most valuable. But our difficulties remain untouched. He tells us that "it is only by an exercise of explanatory reasoning, only by an inferential process resting on the principle of causality, that we are justified in asserting, and are constrained to assert, that God exists".[22] Nevertheless, he agrees with the conclusion reached in the last paragraph: "We do not know that the term 'being' can be predicated of uncreated being until we have proved that uncreated being exists. It is the demonstration of God's existence which necessitates and justifies our use of analogous language about God."[23] How, then, does Fr Daly show that the inferential process on which he insists is a valid one? Unfortunately, and most sur-

---

[20] I have discussed this at length in various places; see, in particular, *The Meaning of Existence* by Dom Mark Pontifex and myself (Longmans, 1953), Pt. II, Ch. II.

[21] *Philosophical Studies*, Maynooth, Ireland. December, 1959, pp. 90–137.

[22] P. 117.

[23] P. 100.

prisingly, he goes on at once to say: "This paper is not concerned to examine the Five Ways of St Thomas, or other
proofs for the existence of God, as such. We assume that the
existence of God can be proved and has been proved...." This
illustrates an attitude of mind which is curiously common
among Thomist writers. Fr Daly does, however, repeat the
usual scholastic doctrine that the meaning of a "pure" attribute
("good", for example) "is not limited to spatio-temporal
objects".[24] I cannot see how we can know this unless we know
that there are objects to which such attributes could be applied,
objects which are not spatio-temporal. It looks as though these
analogous or transcendental notions must *include* a knowledge
of God, and since Fr Daly does not want to demonstrate *them*
inferentially, there seems no point in talking about inference
at all in the present connection.

There is remarkable unanimity on this point both among the
philosophers of religion (apart from the Thomists) and among
the philosophers who are indifferent or hostile to religion, and
one is forced to conclude that the Thomists have no answer to
make.

This chapter has been concerned with the removal of "positivist" obstacles and metaphysical encumbrances. To end it
we may gratefully accept Fr Daly's help in ridding ourselves
of one more encumbrance. That is the doctrine that the proofs
of God's existence, however we may suppose them to work, tell
us nothing about his nature. Fr Daly rightly insists that God
transcends all our knowledge. But he realizes the danger of
such language. Our knowledge of God declares itself to us as
imperfect, but to say that "we do not know in any manner,
respect or degree what God is",[25] as many Thomists do, is to
lapse into complete agnosticism. Fr Daly quotes St Thomas'
own view to this effect: "We could not know *that* God is unless
we had some sort of knowledge, at least a confused knowledge,
of *what* He is."[26] And he takes issue, in particular, with the

[24] P. 126.
[25] P. 130.
[26] P. 132.

fatal ambiguity of Fr Victor White's statement in *God the Unknown*[27]: "It is a sobering thought that, when we talk about God, we do not know what we are talking about." This sort of language is very common among Thomist writers, and Fr Daly shows clearly that it is a misunderstanding of St Thomas. When St Thomas writes that we do not know "what God is", "the phrase has a quite special and technical meaning . . . it means, knowing God as God knows himself".[28] Nobody wants to say that we can do that.

[27] Harvill Press, 1956, p. 51.
[28] P. 130.

CHAPTER IV

REACHING A SOLUTION

In the course of the last chapter we had occasion to note that many modern Thomists combine an "intuitive element" with processes of syllogistic reasoning in describing the ways in which, in their view, we come to know God's existence. If we examine their proposals in detail we shall be brought to the solution which is to be defended in subsequent chapters.

FR JOLIVET ON "INTUITION"

An example of this point of view is to be found in Fr Jolivet's contribution to this series, *The God of Reason*. Proof, he tells us in his Introduction,

> means either to establish by means of experience (direct or indirect) the existence of a fact or being (proof from experience), or else, by a process of reasoning and starting from certain premises, to reach a conclusion which follows necessarily from the premises (proof from reason). [He goes on to say that] there is no proof of God in the first sense. For God, if he exists, is not an object or thing of which we have experience of a scientific type, and no such experience, that is, such as leads to a scientific proof, is possible. If God exists, he cannot be perceived by the senses. Hence, if there is a proof of God, it can only be a proof from reason; it can only take the form of reasoning or of a demonstration, and can only be expressed as a necessary conclusion from the reason.[1]

From this passage we should suppose that Fr Jolivet's approach is on the conventional lines which we have already

[1] *The God of Reason*, volume 15 in this series, p. 9.

discussed. But on the previous page he has spoken of a "notion of God" which is "more intuitive than rational", and on the following page he tells us that "the idea of God as such is, in a sense, previous to the demonstration". He goes on to say: "The process of reasoning only serves to make explicit a sort of intuition, not of God himself, but of the reasons which support the assertion of his existence. Hence it is that the explicit proofs often seem less strong and less satisfying than the intuition which lies behind them." Fr Jolivet further allows that the intuition makes us "aware of God as a spiritual presence" and concludes: "Thus we can see why the traditional proofs have so often met with resistance."

We can indeed. If we are in fact "aware of God as a spiritual presence", then obviously we have no need of further proofs. But that is only the beginning of our difficulties about Fr Jolivet's position. What is an "intuition" of the "reasons for God's existence"? How can it make us "aware of God as a spiritual presence"? Or is this awareness itself the "intuition"? Would not this be an "experience" of God? Yet Fr Jolivet has apparently ruled out the possibility of any "experience" of God from the start.

Here we must face the fact that Fr Jolivet is a philosopher of wide sympathies and considerable penetration whose position is shared by a large number of distinguished writers. I therefore offer my criticism of it with some fear that I may have failed to appreciate its real strength. But, so far as I can see, Fr Jolivet is hovering between two mutually exclusive conclusions. He seems to be impressed by the fact that the traditional arguments are unconvincing, as arguments, for many minds, and concludes that there seems to be some sort of intuition lurking somewhere. He wishes to do justice to the facts, and at the same time wishes to avoid claiming any direct experience of God. Thus he speaks rather vaguely about a "spiritual presence" and stops short of calling an awareness of this presence an "intuition". Instead, he speaks of an intuition which bears not on God himself but on *reasons*.

This seems to enunciate a mere truism. Of course we have

to "intuit", that is, to *see*, that a reason *is* a reason. We have to *see* that a conclusion follows from the premises. But that is precisely the question which is in dispute. *Do* we see the conclusion of the traditional arguments in this way? The appeal to intuition, in fact, may seem to be merely an assertion that the arguments are convincing. But that Fr Jolivet means something else becomes clear when he writes in his Conclusion that the arguments are "contained in this intuition" because it is "only a mass of rapid judgements which seem intuitive".[2] It only *seems* to be an intuition, we may fairly interpret, because the judgements are so natural and spontaneous that we do not recognize them for what they are. And what are they? All we can conclude is that they are not themselves "intuitions", and what else then can they be but inferences? Fr Jolivet is not at all explicit on this crucial point. He writes earlier in the same paragraph: "God is present everywhere, in the light of day, in the darkness of the star-lit night.... Without argument, but only from a natural impulse, the soul perceives in all this the presence of God, that is to say, grasps in a flash its inability to explain anything apart from God." And *how* does it grasp this inability? If this grasping is not itself an intuition of God, what can it be?

In this concluding section[3] of his book Fr Jolivet continues to hover, and he very nearly comes down at times on the "intuitive" side. He speaks of the mistake of supposing "that what gives validity to the proofs of God is their conceptual and logical form, whereas they rest on the need for the absolute, and on the urge of the spirit". And he speaks again of "a spiritual presence" which "can only be grasped by the spirit" and even of a "living experience ... of the presence of God in everything that exists, and especially in the spiritual and moral life". Like so many writers he quotes Pascal's dictum "we should not seek God nor attempt to prove him, if we had not already found him", but, again like so many writers, he is not prepared to accept the full implication of this dictum. He

[2] P. 116.
[3] Pp. 115–18.

makes a final attempt to have it both ways. "Though the intuition of which I have spoken is itself clear and persuasive", our discursive reason has to turn it into "precise concepts" in order to get a proper grasp of it. This seems to me a case of two black riddles making a white answer. If we are to talk about intuition at all, the intuition must provide us with conviction. If it provides only suspicion, an argument not itself demonstrative will not make it a certainty. If the intuition requires support from discursive reason, and discursive reason is helpless without the intuition, it does not seem to make sense to suggest that they can effectively pool their resources. Explicit reasoning can justify implicit reasoning, but it cannot itself give clarity to an intuition. An intuition can come to the rescue of an unconvincing argument, but not by giving strength to it as an argument. An intuition can be prepared for by discursive processes, and it can give rise to harm. And it may be that an intuition cannot fully emerge apart from some form of discourse, but this is not at all the same as saying that it is validated by the "precise concepts" of an argument which is itself invalid. The discovery itself is either indirect, the conclusion of an argument, or it is direct. It cannot be a bit of both. An argument, if valid, needs no support, and, if invalid, is worthless.

Fr Jolivet has enunciated on several occasions, in the body of his book, the doctrine that this "intuition" *contains* processes of reasoning, and he admits that he is not using "intuition" in the strictest sense. We are forced to conclude that the mental processes to which he is referring are merely informal inferences. He thinks that the spontaneous character of these processes makes us doubt whether our formal inferences are really valid, because they seem too cold or abstract. But if they are in fact setting out in a clearer form the movement of thought which has already taken place confusedly, they should provide us simply with a more settled conviction. If this is so, then the appeal to an "intuitive element" seems to have failed in Fr Jolivet's account of it.

FR DANIELOU ON "ENCOUNTER" AND "RELIGIOUS EXPERIENCE"

If we now turn to the similar appeal in Fr Daniélou's *Dieu et Nous*,[4] we shall find much to interest us. In the preface to the book he presents us with the paradox that God is "always unknown", yet everybody knows him. We have already said, in the previous chapter, all that needs to be said of the (at best) highly ambiguous language about an "unknown God" which is fashionable in some quarters; we must suppose that Fr Daniélou is not speaking ambiguously when he tells us that everybody knows God, for he goes on to quote with approval the dictum that there are no atheists, but "only men who believe in God without knowing exactly what they believe". He even adds that "a little child knows him, perhaps before knowing its mother", and in his first chapter he tells us that "before he spoke through Moses and Jesus Christ, God spoke once to all men through the cosmos and the conscience".[5] In his second chapter he allows that the "encounter" with God is a personal event which is "never a development of pure reason".[6] But he adds at once that this "encounter" must be rationally justified if we are to be assured that it is not an illusion.

Once again there seems to be an attempt to have it both ways. If there is indeed an "encounter" with God which is "never a development of pure reason", we can assure ourselves that it has taken place only by inspecting this situation with all possible care. An encounter is a matter of fact, not of logic; there can be no proof of it other than our awareness of it. If the "encounter" proves to provide us only with a "suspicion", and if it is only its rational justification which provides us with conviction, then the "encounter" has been only the occasion of the conviction; the rational justification has been its cause. And

---

[4] Grasset, Paris, 1956. English Trans., *God and Us*, London, Mowbrays, 1957; American edn, *God and the Ways of Knowing*, New York, Meridian Books.

[5] P. 16.

[6] Pp. 45-6.

what can rational justification be, we are forced to repeat, but an inference? That this is the ultimate direction of the writer's thought is indicated by a passage a little later in the same chapter in which God is said to be "postulated by the existence of contingent being and by the existence of morality".[7] There is no attempt to produce a syllogistic argument, but it is difficult to see how anything else can be envisaged in such a context. The "encounter" has now dropped out of the picture.

Fr Daniélou's account is of service to us not only because it introduces us to the language of "encounter" and contains the suggestion that atheists may be in fact theists in disguise, but also, as we shall now see, because it puts before us once more the question of "religious experience". Throughout the book Fr Daniélou rejects "religious experience" as the basis of religion. This he describes as "pre-eminently subjective".[8] Its certitude, he goes on to say, is incommunicable, and an alleged knowledge of God thus becomes a mere accident of temperament, which can be easily written off by psychologists as a mere "projection". We have had occasion to note already that the word "experience" is a slippery one. If it is used to mean a merely subjective feeling, then, as we saw, it is clearly of no interest to us here. A merely subjective feeling can make no claims about objective truth. But it is highly undesirable to restrict the word "experience" to this usage. If there is an "encounter" with God, we must call it an "experience"; if we are unwilling to do so, we shall be understood to mean that it is an *unconscious* affair, and that is equally of no interest. What, then, is this "encounter" of which Fr Daniélou speaks? If we are to make anything of it it must be an *intellectual experience*. To this we shall return before the end of the chapter.

[7] Pp. 47–8.
[8] P. 45.

FR EDWARD SILLEM AND A "DIALECTICAL WAY OF THINKING"

Three further examples of the attempt to compromise must now be given. Fr Edward Sillem has written[9] of a "natural and non-syllogistic universal way of thinking about God". This begins with the supposition that there might be "some being not of this world and independent of it . . . the only real reality after all" and produces "the possibility of there being a God". This is a "dialectical way of thinking", and engenders "a subjective certitude in the minds of ordinary people which is not infrequently objectively verifiable, and this is exactly the case with the certitude they can have of God's existence". Unfortunately Fr Sillem has not yet told us in what this "dialectical way of thinking" consists, except that we use it "when we are dealing in ordinary life with matters which touch us very closely and especially in forming our opinion of other people". It is certainly not, in Fr Sillem's view, an "encounter" with God. And it is not syllogistic, despite the fact that, according to Fr Sillem, the philosopher may then come along and produce a syllogistic justification of it, the second premiss of which is that "contingent beings must ultimately be caused by non-contingent beings"—a premiss which, as we have seen, will be accepted only by those who are already, in effect, theists. Fr Sillem, however, says that "a professed atheist can understand what we mean by the metaphysical contingency of things even though he denies that the expression 'necessary being' has any meaning", and he also says that "our idea of necessary being is derived from and logically dependent on our idea of contingent being". But he has not yet shown the logical nexus between the idea of contingent being which the professed atheist is supposed to understand and the idea of necessary being. How can the idea of necessary being be *generated* by the idea of non-necessary being? Isn't this to make the greater emerge from the less with a vengeance? Mustn't the idea of necessary being be somehow *given* along with the idea of non-necessary

[9] *The Downside Review*, Jan. 1958, pp. 49–50.

being? If in fact we are to possess either of these ideas, mustn't they arise at the same time?

But we have been over this ground often enough. What is to be noted here more particularly is that Fr Sillem produces his syllogism for the ordinary man as showing "not the line of reasoning which has led him to conclude that necessary Being exists, but the impersonal, logical inevitability with which the conclusion ... follows from the metaphysical premisses ...". The admission that the existence of God is not in fact found syllogistically is offset by the claim that it can be syllogistically justified. But the attempt at compromise has produced nothing which is capable of providing conviction syllogistically—or non-syllogistically.

AN INTRODUCTION TO THE AUGUSTINIAN TRADITION: FR DEFEVER AND FR CAYRE

Our second example comes from a distinguished little work, *La Preuve Réelle de Dieu*, by Fr Defever, S.J., continuing the thought of the great Jesuit philosopher, Fr Maréchal. "What guarantees God's transcendence—the turning point of the whole argument—is the intimate experience, made available to us by 'total reflection', of the transcendence of our powers of affirmation in regard to all determinations of possible objects";[10] this means that in knowing some particular object we may become aware, if we reflect upon the situation with sufficient attention, that it is only a *particular* object, and that our power of knowledge transcends all such objects. Fr Defever writes that, although we have no intuition of *God* in the strict sense, this "intuition of our act of transcending the finite" is a "true presence of God" without which we should have no knowledge of God at all; thanks to which our knowledge of him is direct, personal, enriching the human personality.[11] Indeed, "this proof coincides with our reality as we make it to be if we are faithful to ourselves. . .".[12] This is, no doubt, some-

[10] P. 124.
[11] P. 107.
[12] P. 94.

what obscure at the moment; I hope it will become clearer later. What should be clear is that our knowledge of God, although mediated by the "intuition of our act of transcending the finite", has a character of directness about it in this account. The "intuitive element" has moved to the front of the stage, and the attempt at compromise has been virtually abandoned (although there is a good deal about deductive processes and metaphysical principles in Fr Defever's book which is hard to reconcile with the quoted passages).

The final example introduces us to the tradition of thought on which the constructive proposals of the present book will largely rely. This is the Augustinian tradition, taken up in various ways by St Anselm, by St Bonaventure, by Pascal, by Newman, by Maurice Blondel in our time and by a host of others. It is embedded in the Thomist tradition, as may appear from passages already quoted, but overlaid by other elements. Fr Defever has almost come back to it; Fr Jolivet, an authority on St Augustine, is drawing on it when he speaks of a "presence of God" (he gives a useful account of it in *The God of Reason*). What has been said so far about an "intuitive element" has prepared the way for it, although the knowledge of God which is to be claimed should not, in my opinion, be called an "intuition". I shall call it an "apprehension". The "apprehension" can come about in various ways, but the form in which St Augustine prefers to discuss it is that which is to be found in the famous second book of his *De Libero Arbitrio*, and we have now to see how St Augustine's argument is summarized by the patristic and Augustinian scholar, Fr Cayré.[13] He puts it into the following syllogistic form:

If there is something higher than the human mind, then this is God.

[13] In *Dieu présent dans la vie de l'esprit* (Desclée, 1951), p. 148. In what follows I am quoting from the notice of this book by Dom Mark Pontifex in *The Downside Review*, 1952, p. 339. See also Dom Mark's discussion of the matter in *The Problem of Free Choice*, his translation of the *De Libero Arbitrio* (Ancient Christian Writers XXII, Westminster, Md, Newman Press, and London, Longmans, 1955).

There is Perfect Truth which is above the human mind.
So God exists, he is Truth.

But what St Augustine in fact does is to "take instances in
which we recognize truth, and to show that in these the truth
is unchangeable and eternal". His method consists in "analysing what we are aware of from the beginning ... in making
explicit what was at first implicit. ... Thus it is not a question
with St Augustine of starting from some fact and then, by
means of a general principle, claiming to find that this fact
involves another which is in no way contained in the first. It is
a question of realizing clearly what we were aware of at first
obscurely, namely, that Perfect Truth exists".

Fr Cayré, it seems, has thought it necessary to extract a syllogism from St Augustine's discussion, although the conclusion
itself does not seem to have been reached syllogistically by
St Augustine himself. St Augustine, like his master Plato, is not
a systematically consistent philosopher, and his language does
at times suggest a syllogistic method. But it is pretty clear that
his mind moves, in this matter, on other lines. It appears to be
Fr Cayré's anxiety to make St Augustine's "proof" acceptable
to the Thomist establishment that has led him to combine a
syllogistic interpretation of the "proof" with the admission that
it contains an "intuitive note, a mediate and indirect one, but
a real one". This is so because "God is essentially Being, Truth
and Goodness", and "the soul (*l'esprit*) is the image of God
par excellence, and we may in some sense contemplate him in
this image better than in any other object".[14] But, if this is so,
there seems to be no need for compromise with methods of
argument which involve abstract principles and syllogistic
processes.

We have thus been led to the Augustinian notion of *contuitio*.
We shall not be concerned with the contexts in which it is
presented to us by St Augustine; these often contain elements
which are irrelevant for our purposes. It is simply the fact
that we "in some sense contemplate" God in the human soul

[14] *Op cit.*, pp. 151–2.

which will be our presiding theme. It is a mediate contemplation in so far as it is only in his action on the soul that we
know him; for example, when our minds are employing the
standard of truth, God is acting upon them, and we are in
reality acknowledging this in accepting that standard. This
element of "mediacy" is a reason for avoiding the word "intuition", which implies an immediate vision. Fr Cayré retains
the word "intuitive" but discards the word "direct" in his
account of it as quoted above; it seems that we should reverse
the process. We must be in direct touch in some sense with
an object of contemplation even if we have no immediate vision
of it. This distinction between "direct" and "immediate" is
made by Canon Nédoncelle, for example, in *La réciprocité des
consciences*.[15] And it is this mediate but direct awareness of
God which I shall call our "apprehension" of him.

Let us pause for a moment to take stock of the position. It
might seem that it is high time for me to elaborate and defend
this doctrine and to resume the metaphysical analysis on which
we had embarked when, in the middle of the last chapter, we
were faced by the massive obstacle of the syllogism (that
analysis, it will now be seen, was already adumbrating the
Augustinian solution). But there is so much prejudice against
allowing any sort of directness in our knowledge of God that
it will be wiser first to show that there is support for it. It is
indeed abundantly supported by both philosophers and theologians. In a book of this kind it is obviously impossible to give
even the most summary account of what I have called the
Augustinian tradition. In this chapter I shall simply illustrate it
by a brief reference to St Bonaventure; there will be further
references to it in other chapters. In the two following chapters
I shall adduce support from recent books so that the position of
the question in our own time will be made clear, at least to
some extent—it will have appeared that this has been my intention also in regard to the preliminary questions which have
engaged us. We are dealing with an actual question; it must be

[15] 1942; p. 107.

seen for what it is and discussed in the language of our con-
temporaries. It must be understood, then, that in the next two
chapters we shall be discussing in a quite general way the
possibility of a certain directness in our knowledge of God and
shall not confine ourselves to the forms in which it commonly
appears in "Augustinian writers".

M. GILSON AND ST BONAVENTURE

But the standpoint of one such writer may be indicated at
once in the words of M. Gilson—it would be absurd to attempt
any fresh formulation of St Bonaventure's thought when we
have so high an authority at our disposal. In this passage from
The Philosophy of St Bonaventure M. Gilson is referring to
the famous "ontological argument" of St Anselm, to which we
shall soon return: [16]

> But St Anselm's argument is practically identical in St Bona-
> venture's eyes with St Augustine's argument from the existence
> of truth. This is so not only because truth is in fact God him-
> self, but also because each particular truth implies the existence
> of an absolute truth whereof it is the effect. Therefore to affirm
> any individual truth at all is to affirm the existence of God....
> It is not in virtue of a purely dialectical analysis of abstract con-
> cepts that we can, starting from no judgement at all, proceed
> immediately to infer the existence of God; it is not simply a
> logical repugnance that makes it impossible for us to deny the
> existence of God without contradicting ourselves; this repug-
> nance is but a sign of a metaphysical impossibility with which
> we are in conflict. If God is present in our soul by the truth
> which we discover therein, how can we deny him in his own
> name? Since we know nothing save by his light, how can we
> affirm in the name of that light that the first light does not
> exist? This radical impossibility of denying God is therefore the
> effect left on the face of our soul by the divine light. [17]

[16] But it may be noted at once that this argument is coming more
and more to be understood not as a "proof" but as a way of pointing
to the presence of God in the soul—St Anselm is in the Augustinian
tradition.

[17] Pp. 131–2, Eng. trans., Sheed and Ward, London, 1938.

M. Gilson goes on to say that the starting point of St Bonaventure's whole argument is the doctrine of "a natural aptitude
of the soul to perceive God", and this leads him to some important conclusions: "This definite orientation of St Bonaventure's thought dooms to futility any attempt to bring it
within the same historic framework as that of St Thomas."
When St Thomas speaks of an "implicit" knowledge of God,
M. Gilson assures us, he can only be referring to

> something undetermined to which some further addition will
> give determination.... It is impossible to suppose that any
> knowledge whatsoever should be originally given to us in the
> intellect itself ... it is a series of determinations, added to the
> idea of being by the intellect, in the course of the exploration
> of the world of sense, which is to determine and build up the idea
> of God.... From the beginning to the end of his career St
> Thomas never taught otherwise: intellectual light is a means
> of knowing, it is never an object known. A man may maintain
> the contrary and call himself a Thomist, but he is thinking as
> an Augustinian ... the implicit, which attains determination in
> St Thomas by the intellectual exploration of the sensible, attains
> determination in St Bonaventure by a deeper exploration of
> itself, by a progressive and increasingly powerful recognition
> of the intimate relationship which binds the human soul to
> God.[18] [Finally] St Bonaventure dares to maintain that the
> simplest explanation of our idea of God is God. An idea which
> comes neither from things nor from ourselves can come from
> none other than God; it is in us as the mark left by God upon
> his work; it is therefore eminently qualified to attest irrefutably
> the evidence of its object. The presence of the idea of God in
> the human soul would be unintelligible if it did not manifest the
> presence there, by way of truth, of a God really existent.[19]

St Anselm's argument, to which the last of these passages
alludes once more, took the following form: we have in our
minds an idea of a being than which none greater can be conceived; but if this being were only an idea and not a reality it
would not be a being than which none greater can be conceived,

[18] Pp. 132–6.
[19] Pp. 137–8.

precisely because it would lack reality. The fallacy in this argument is apparent, and was pointed out by St Thomas as well as by Kant; if we start with a mere idea we cannot convert it into a reality by a mere device of logic. St Bonaventure avoids this mistake. Again in M. Gilson's words: "The idea is for him simply the mode whereby the being is present to his thought."[20] There is still a widespread impression that the evidence for God's existence can always be reduced in one way or another to St Anselm's "ontological argument". This was Kant's contention. It must be stressed, then, that St Bonaventure's position does not in any way involve this argument.

But we shall not take over St Bonaventure's position without criticism. An innate idea of God—for that is what it amounts to—seems unplausible, as it stands. But that the fact of knowledge itself, the claim of truth, may prove, in certain contingencies, to reveal God's presence, is open to discussion. That there is a tradition in favour of it has been made clear by the words of our greatest historian of medieval philosophy, and it has also been made clear that it is, in his opinion, irreconcilable with the Thomist tradition.[21]

[20] P. 129.
[21] Fr de Lubac in *The Discovery of God* takes a different view, suggesting that St Thomas is really in fundamental agreement with St Bonaventure. But he has not made this out. I shall refer to this book later.

CHAPTER V

SUPPORT FOR THE
SOLUTION IN ENGLISH

Philosophers of religion have had an uphill task during the last quarter of a century, but some of them, at least, have been quite undeterred by the situation. In this chapter I shall refer to a number of these who all lend their support to the contention that there must be a character of directness about our knowledge of God, despite the fact that it is not an immediate vision—it is an obscure, though genuine, apprehension. Nearly all these writers are non-Catholics. This is not surprising when we consider the relatively small number of English Catholic writers in this field. But we must not gloss over the fact that there is a marked tendency among English-speaking Catholics to regard any departure from the Thomist positions with disapproval and even with alarm. This is not so in France to anything like the same extent, and we shall find plenty of examples in the next chapter of French Catholics who provide support for the present thesis. It must not be thought that agreement with any of these writers—English or French—extends necessarily beyond the particular field of inquiry which is our concern. Their approaches to the question may differ from mine in many respects; so may the consequences which they draw from their answers to the question. The point is that it is in each case the same answer.

PRINCIPAL JOHN BAILLIE: ON MORAL OBLIGATION AND ON THOMIST ANALOGY

The first of these writers whom we shall consider has been criticized for overlooking or misunderstanding the Thomist distinction between natural and supernatural knowledge, and I have no wish to contest this criticism. But his positive teaching on the points here at issue seems to me, in the main, acceptable. Principal John Baillie's book *Our Knowledge of God* was first published in 1939,[1] and it has been reprinted since seven times. He takes his stand resolutely with the "Augustinians".

We are rejecting logical argument of any kind as the first chapter of our theology or as representing the process by which God comes to be known.... We are thus directly challenging St Thomas' doctrine ... and are allying ourselves with that other strain in mediaeval thought ... the doctrine represented by St Bonaventure's dictum that God is present to the soul itself (*Deus praesens est ipsi animae*).[2] [Of St Anselm's "proof" Principal Baillie writes that] it attempts only to show that to form the conception of God in our minds is already to believe in his reality. [And he continues:] It might therefore be supposed that, just as the intention of St Anselm's proof is confessedly not to lead us to believe in God, so also its intention is not to show us *why* we believe in him. That this was St Anselm's own reading of his proof does not, however, appear. And it is just here, I believe, that we must part company with him. No proof of God's existence can help us to understand our faith in him, or can in the last resort do anything but hinder such understanding, *if* it be true that it is not by a process of inference that our faith has actually been reached. It is not as the result of an inference of any kind, whether explicit or implicit, whether laboriously excogitated or swiftly intuited, that the knowledge of God's reality comes to us.[3]

[1] Oxford University Press.
[2] P. 152.
[3] P. 143.

This I accept in principle[4] with the proviso, already suggested, that the knowledge of God which is accessible to all men in all circumstances is not, as the writer goes on at once to call it, a "direct personal encounter with Him in the Person of our Lord Jesus Christ", but an awareness of him which is no more than an awareness of the transcendent Infinite and a summons to a fuller supernatural knowledge, the knowledge of faith.

With this distinction made, we may also accept, it seems to me, Principal Baillie's account of a knowledge of God "which, being more deep-seated than any opinion, may to some extent coexist even with the opinion that we have no knowledge of his existence", although he goes too far, I think, in claiming (or appearing to claim) that such knowledge is naturally enjoyed by all men and at all times, although it is not recognized as such. This is surely contrary to the facts, and I prefer to say that it must be accessible in some way and at some time for all men. (There is no question of unconscious knowledge; the professing atheist has knowledge of God, but supposes it to be something else.) But the most notable feature of this knowledge, in Principal Baillie's account of it, is its identification with the consciousness of *obligation*: "Kant himself (in the *Opus Posthumum*) is found veering round towards the view that God, instead of being merely reached by deduction from the profound experiences of the moral life, is himself actually present to us in these experiences."[5] We may doubt whether Kant ever reached the conclusion that we can have direct knowledge of a transcendent God, but there is, happily, no doubt about Principal Baillie's own view of the matter.

At the end of the book he permits himself to speak of an "argument" in this connection—and rightly, for the analysis of experience on which he is engaged is a rational, though not an inferential, activity:

[4] Although I shall contend that the traditional arguments, *properly envisaged*, are far from useless.
[5] P. 131.

This argument would, as I conceive it, consist in the defence of two propositions: first, that *no obligation can be absolute which does not derive from the Absolute* (or unconditioned which does not derive from the Unconditioned) ... and second, that since morality is a function of personality, we can feel no moral obligation to an Absolute which is not apprehended by us as a personal being.... The will which we are called upon to obey is indeed another Will than ours, yet a Will in obedience to which we can alone find our true selfhood and our wills their real freedom.[6]

The whole context of this passage deserves the closest attention of all students of the philosophy of religion and indeed of all educated religious persons. It leads to the conclusion that our "ideal of personality" can have its source only in God. And "what is true of personality is true also of goodness, as well as of such conceptions as infinity, eternity, omniscience and omnipotence. All these conceptions we certainly possess, yet it is clear that we do not find them in ourselves or anywhere in the created world.... It must be that we have some direct knowledge of Another who is Uncreated."[7]

This leads Principal Baillie to a final repudiation of Thomist analogy:

It is greatly to be deplored that the Roman Catholic thought of our time, by regarding itself as committed to the defence of St Thomas' position in this matter (while thinking to protect itself, as it no doubt successfully does, against the worst), is at the same time shutting itself out from the best of post-Renaissance thought.... What is false is that the comparison moves from man to God, instead of from God to man. Such a view, if consistently carried out, is bound to end in anthropomorphism.[8]

But, as we saw in the last chapter, there is another account of Thomist analogy (not, unfortunately, very much in currency) which escapes these strictures.

[6] Pp. 244–6.
[7] Pp. 251–2.
[8] P. 254.

Principal Baillie quotes a great many authors in support of his position; here it must be enough to mention one of them. Dr H. H. Farmer, until recently Norris-Hulse Professor of Divinity at Cambridge, has written several books on our subject, and two extracts from *The World and God*[9] must suffice to indicate their general tenour:

> We suggest that always at the heart of man's religious response to this world there can be discerned (a) an awareness of unconditional demand; (b) an awareness of man's well-being as somehow bound up with his obedience to that demand; (c) an awareness of the final reality of his world meeting him in such absolute demand and proffered succour; (d) a certain reverberation of feeling of the nature of worship or awe....[10] Only by discerning the unity of the world can the inner conflicts of the personality be resolved, and only as the inner conflicts of the personality are being resolved can the unity of the world be discerned. It is a single unitary response in which the objective unity meets the need for wholeness in an emancipating awareness of God.[11]

Thus Dr Farmer is led to conclude that man's relationship to God is "immediate, yet not mediated".[12] "Immediate" here is clearly the same as "direct" in my language.

DR LANGMEAD CASSERLEY: ON SELF-CONSCIOUSNESS

Dr Langmead Casserley's book *The Christian in Philosophy* also belongs to the Augustinian tradition. "The essence of Augustine's theism", he tells us, is that "immediate self-consciousness is not a consciousness of the self alone.... It carries with it an immediate apprehension of the Creator."[13] He continues:

[9] Nisbet & Co., 2nd edn 1936 (reprinted 1948).
[10] P. 28.
[11] P. 43.
[12] P. 76.
[13] Faber and Faber, London, 1949, p. 44.

This insistence that Christian theism is primarily a matter of self-consciousness, rather than a metaphysic of nature, is one of two ways of understanding and expressing Christian philosophy which run side by side, and in strong contrast with one another, throughout the later history of Christian thought. In our own time this philosophy of self-consciousness has begun to be called "existentialism", the term used by the most brilliant and thorough-going exponent of such an approach to God and faith, Sören Kierkegaard.[14]

It is perhaps unfortunate that Dr Casserley has adopted the word "existentialism" here, since it has come to cover a great variety of doctrines, many of them irrationalist or impenetrable. But, as we shall see later, some of the writers known as "existentialists" have indeed something to offer us. It is, according to Dr Casserley, "the Augustinian, existentialist succession" which has the true claim to be regarded as the "perennial philosophy" of Western Europe.[15]

Dr Casserley concludes, much like Principal Baillie, that St Anselm's purpose was to demonstrate "not that God exists but that all rational beings believe in his existence".[16] He, too, contrasts St Thomas with St Bonaventure:

> In general St Thomas maintains, like all Aristotelians . . . the impossibility in this life of any direct apprehension of God. . . . The Augustinians, on the other hand, were always emphatic in accepting the possibility of at least some degree of real apprehension even in this life. For St Bonaventure, for example, the aim of the human mind is never merely to know God but always, and more urgently, to see Him; and it is this latter desire which for him provides the motive power of Christian philosophy as truly as of Christian life and prayer.[17]

Dr Casserley proceeds to claim Descartes, Malebranche, Berkeley and Kant as members of the Augustinian "succession". For Kant, he tells us, "it is moral experience, but here we begin to

[14] P. 45.
[15] P. 50.
[16] P. 60.
[17] P. 75.

use Augustinian rather than Kantian terminology, which disciplines and deepens self-consciousness to the point at which it becomes metaphysically conscious and significant".[18] He quotes Newman's contrast between inference and assent: "We may call it then the normal state of Inference to apprehend propositions as notions; and we may call it the normal state of Assent to apprehend propositions as things. If notional apprehension is most congenial to Inference, real apprehension will be the most natural concomitant on Assent."[19] Moreover, Dr Casserley concludes, "there is absolutely no possibility that the realm of inference can ever be extended to include sheer singularity within its range" whereas "the response to the singular is the characteristic spiritual act, the fundamental theme of a genuine and satisfying existentialist philosophy, the true and necessary act of faith".[20] So the parallel with Principal Baillie, whose book is not mentioned by Dr Casserley, extends also to the blurring of the distinction, emphasized above, between "supernatural faith" and a "natural apprehension".

DR AUSTIN FARRER: ON THE TRADITIONAL ARGUMENTS

The most massive contribution to the debate in the period under review was *Finite and Infinite*[21] by Dr Austin Farrer, now Warden of Keble. He disposes of the question about inference at once: "God is not an instance of a type of being elsewhere directly experienced"[22] and "it is not merely that (as St Thomas says) he cannot be demonstrated *a priori*. . . . He cannot be demonstrated *a posteriori* either, i.e. from his effects, because we must first know that these are effects, and effects of a perfectly unique activity. But to know that they are effects in the relevant sense is to know the nature of the activity."[23]

[18] P. 130.
[19] *Essay in Aid of a Grammar of Assent*, p. 40.
[20] P. 194.
[21] Dacre Press, London, 1943.
[22] P. 4.
[23] P. 7.

So "the theist's first argument is a statement; he exhibits his account of God active in the world and the world existing in God, that others may recognize it to be the account of what they themselves apprehend...."[24] It is impossible to summarize Dr Farrer's argument, but very roughly it works out to this: that we apprehend God *in* the created relationships of which the traditional arguments are statements, but these statements can never be informative without the apprehension: "We must have direct awareness of the [creative] activity."[25] Moreover "we have direct insight into our own activity alone,"[26] which brings us back to the Augustinian tradition. In fact the greater part of this impressive work is devoted to a vindication of the "self" against the "dissolving" techniques of the Positivists, of which we have already said all that we have space to say. At the end of the book Dr Farrer returns to the subject of the traditional arguments and in particular to that which bases itself on the distinction between essence and existence in created beings. Such arguments, he says, in effect, do *point* to the conclusion. They are all attempting to show that finite being is non-self-explanatory. But "there is no *reason* why it is ... non-self-explanatory; it just is so, and this must be appreciated".[27]

PROF. H. D. LEWIS: ON RELIGIOUS EXPERIENCE

We may now turn to the most recent of these major contributions, Professor H. D. Lewis's *Our Experience of God*.[28] The traditional arguments fail, he considers, "in trying to break into a series of steps what is in fact one insight and also in seeking to start from purely finite factors and reason to conclusions about the infinite.... It is true that we do proceed from finite facts, and from any such facts as you please, to some reality 'beyond' or 'other than' these. But the movement

[24] P. 9.
[25] P. 61.
[26] P. 44.
[27] P. 265.
[28] Allen & Unwin, 1959.

of thought which proceeds in this way is unique and has no strict analogy elsewhere." The traditional arguments, however, are valuable because they reveal to us "the movement of thought which lies behind and makes them plausible". Prof. Lewis suggests that those who find the "argument from design" impressive "are combining with it the initial insight into the inevitability of there being some complete and unconditional source of the realities we actually meet; and to this extent it also converges on the insight which lies behind the other arguments".[29] At first sight we might suppose that this insight (which Prof. Lewis calls, unfortunately, I think, an "intuition") is not precisely an apprehension of God, a direct cognitive contact of some kind, but only an insight into the "inevitability" of God. And the contrast which he makes between "intuition" and "religious experience" may seem to bear this out. But it becomes clear eventually that Prof. Lewis does not intend such a distinction. He lays it down that "our apprehension of supreme being is personal from the start" (i.e. apprehensive of a person), and later writes unambiguously of "an intuition of the being of God as the unconditional source of all other being".[30]

There is much that is of great value in this book, and the following paragraph is of particular service to us at this stage:

It is of extreme importance, for the proper commendation of religion today as well as for the enrichment that comes through right understanding of it, that it be made clear that the "beyond" which we seek must also be found somehow within. It is this paradox of course that the positivist challenges us to sustain, inviting us either to abandon religion or to conceive of it entirely in humanist terms. But we must hold boldly to the peculiar character of religion that it concerns what is in one sense altogether beyond, and in another sense altogether within. Those who fail to appreciate this are tempted to look altogether beyond themselves and their environment, to peer into the void, and of course they see nothing. They apprehend the ordinary world

[29] Pp. 41–3.
[30] P. 144.

about them and nothing besides. They declare that religion means nothing to them, and they report their state truly. But what they should be urged to do is to look into themselves and the world for evidence within these of what is also altogether beyond them.[31]

And we may also usefully take note of the remark: "even the very partial acquaintance which the casual student or amateur gains with early religion shows that, in its general form, it presents, *to those who consider it from within a religious life of their own* (my italics), elements identical with our experience of God."[32]

Again there is the emphasis on knowledge of the "self", although this is bound up, as in Dr Farrer's account, with our knowledge of the world outside. There is only one definite disagreement in this book with the positions which I am advocating about the apprehension of God. Prof. Lewis holds that it is possible to accept the objectivity of ethics and to acknowledge the absoluteness of obligation while at the same time maintaining an atheist or agnostic standpoint.[33] I shall argue in detail later that such acknowledgment is itself an apprehension of God.

DR E. C. MASCALL AND DOM MARK PONTIFEX: ON MEDIATE APPREHENSION

The philosophers so far discussed in this chapter are non-Catholics. And it may now be pointed out that there is a long-standing tradition among Anglican writers that the apprehension of God is at the root of all our thinking. Mr S. L. Bethell in *The Cultural Revolution of the Seventeenth Century*[34] has discussed this in a particularly relevant way, quoting Stillingfleet's words "the foundation of certainty lies in the necessary existence of a being absolutely perfect"[35] and relating them

[31] Pp. 58–9.
[32] P. 83.
[33] Pp. 265–6.
[34] Dennis Dobson, London, 1951, pp. 30 f.
[35] Origines Sacrae (1662), p. 230.

to my own views as expressed some fifteen years ago.[36] The philosopher who has been chiefly instrumental in propagating these views, and more particularly the almost identical views of Dom Mark Pontifex, is the Anglican Dr E. C. Mascall. The development of his thought is of peculiar significance and must be briefly sketched.

Dr Mascall is well known as the most thoroughgoing Thomist among Anglican philosophers. Yet in his first book on our subject, *He Who Is*,[37] he concluded that syllogistic statement in natural theology is "primarily a device for persuading our minds to apprehend finite beings in their radical finitude and thus ... to apprehend the existence of God who is their Creator". He emphasized, however, that this is not to claim a direct apprehension of God for our natural powers, although "if we perceive finite beings as they actually are we shall in perceiving them recognize the existence of God whom we cannot perceive".[38] This is a little ambiguous. In *Existence and Analogy*[39] he tells us that "the primary requirement if we are to pass from the recognition of the finite to the affirmation of the infinite is not that we shall be skilled in the manipulation of Aristotelian logic but that we shall grasp in its ontological reality the act by which finite existents exist. And then we shall affirm God by recognizing him ... as the primary agent of the act by which finite beings exist."[40] This leads to the conclusion that "the apprehension of God as the cause of finite beings, upon which the whole of this existentialist approach is based, is not a mere apprehension of God's existence; it is a recognition of his nature as well".[41] This is a firmer statement. And it is in this second book that Dr Mascall refers on several occasions to a formula which he has often repeated in later books from Dom Mark Pontifex's *The Existence of God*:[42] the

[36] See articles in *The Downside Review*, April and October, 1946.
[37] Longmans, London, 1943, p. 192.
[38] Pp. 73–4.
[39] Longmans, London, 1949.
[40] P. 77.
[41] P. 123.
[42] Longmans, London, 1946.

direct object of our experience is "effect-implying–cause"—that is to say, when we begin to think about ourselves and our environment we find ourselves operating with a double concept.

Dom Mark put it as follows: "We can focus our attention on the idea of the source of being as that element in the background of the double concept, effect-implying-cause, with which we start, but if we try to bring it into the foreground and isolate it and look at it directly, we find ourselves looking, not at the first cause as such, but once again at a limited essence with the cause in the background."[43] That is why the apprehension of God (of God's nature, not only of his exist-ence, whatever that might mean) is not to be called an "in-tuition"; it is only "in the background" of creatures that we know him, but then we *do* know him *in* his creatures.

Dr Mascall accepts this position unequivocally in his later writings. In *Words and Images*,[44] perhaps the most readable of his philosophical books, he frankly admits, for the first time as far as I am aware, that the difficulty for the defenders of syllogistic inference is "how to prove the truth of the major premiss without already begging the conclusion", and he con-tinues:

> I for one cannot see how this can be done. There is, how-ever, another school of thought of which, in spite of their differ-ences on points of detail, Dr A. M. Farrer, Dom Mark Pontifex and Dom Illtyd Trethowan are representative, according to which the function of the arguments is to direct the mind to certain features of finite beings which can easily be overlooked and from which the existence of God can be seen without a discursive process. There is no question of asserting that, in this movement, we have a direct and immediate apprehension of God; direct, if you like, but not immediate, for it is mediated by and in our apprehension of finite beings.[45]

Dr Mascall thus accepts the distinction between "direct" and "immediate" with which this chapter is principally con-cerned. It is to be noted, moreover, that in this passage he is

[43] *Op. cit.*, p. 32.
[44] Longmans, London, 1957.
[45] Pp. 84–5.

defending "natural theology"—that is, he also accepts the distinction between a "natural apprehension" of God and supernatural faith.

Here I should perhaps explain that the differences between Dr Farrer, Dom Mark and myself do not bear so much on the apprehension of God (the differences in this regard are, I think, at bottom purely verbal) as on the appropriate means of provoking it, or perhaps merely on the audiences which we have in mind. The sort of analysis which Dr Farrer conducts is one which is not likely to commend itself except to professional philosophers. And Dom Mark, although he avoids complexities and technicalities, uses for his own purposes the language of scholasticism. Both of them would agree that knowledge of the world outside is of little use for metaphysical purposes *apart* from knowledge of the "self", but they (perhaps Dr Mascall also) would probably say that I take my stand too exclusively upon the latter. For in general I think it less helpful to conduct the analysis in abstract terms than to adopt the method which M. Gabriel Marcel has called that of "concrete metaphysics".

The point may be brought out by a passage from Dr Mascall's *Via Media*:[46]

> Some modern scholastics have indeed gone so far as to maintain that, in the case of finite beings, the act of existence does not merely *imply* dependence upon God but is flatly identical with it. This point of view has been vigorously argued by Dom Mark Pontifex and Dom Illtyd Trethowan in their book *The Meaning of Existence*. They remark that, while existence is a common characteristic of all finite beings, it cannot be a constituent of their nature, since the nature of any one of them would be precisely the same whether they existed or not. What, then, they ask, can this characteristic be which applies to every one of them, but belongs to the nature of none of them? It can, they reply, only be their relation of dependence upon God. Hence, when we apprehend the existence of any object in its full ontological force, when, that is, we have learnt *to see the object*

[46] Longmans, London, 1956, p. 29.

as it really is, we simultaneously though mediately, apprehend its creative cause, God.

In fact, in my contribution to *The Meaning of Existence*,[47] I suggest that the distinction between "essence" (or "nature") and "existence" leads to unnecessary metaphysical difficulties, while agreeing that the usage of the word "existence" does *point* to the "common aspect of derivation from a single source".

MR E. I. WATKIN AND FR O. HARDWICKE: ON "MONSTRATION"

For reasons mentioned at the beginning of this chapter it is not easy to find support for a "direct" knowledge of God in books by English Catholics. We may quote Mr E. I. Watkin, who has urged for many years that we should speak of "monstrations", not of "demonstrations", of God's existence: "the existence of God is not demonstrated, as demonstration is normally understood, namely as a process of cogent but non-intuitive reasoning. It is monstrated to contemplative intellection."[48] But examples of such a thesis are to be found for the most part in article-form. A particularly close coincidence with the views here advocated is to be found in Mr (now Fr) Owen Hardwicke's article "Dr Hawkins and the Essentials of Theism".[49] Some quotations from it will conveniently end this chapter:

> The question is whether the logical method used by Dr Hawkins and other Thomists is adequate to overcome the difficulties of those who are genuinely puzzled. . . . The natural theologian needs to make it quite clear that the finite/Infinite, conditioned/Unconditioned division is not a mere logical one, but is a distinction open to discovery in one's own experience. . . . It is, I believe, Dr Hawkins' view that we must insist to all

[47] In Pt II, Chapter I.
[48] *The Philosophy of Form*, Sheed and Ward, London, 3rd edn, 1950, p. 289.
[49] *The Downside Review*, 1950, pp. 46 f, reviewing Dr Hawkins' *The Essentials of Theism*, Sheed and Ward, London, 1949.

and sundry that it is possible to deduce from certain experiences, say that of change, the existence of an Infinite Unchanged
Changer. Some of those, of whom I am one, who cannot follow
this sort of argument, believe that there is a more ready-to-hand
way of reaching the Infinite by an analysis of experience. We
cannot argue from finite to Infinite, unless we really see that
things *are* finite—and that means seeing them as dependent on
the Infinite. No one, I hope, would doubt the validity of the
distinction between the sensible and the intellectual: but intellectual knowledge operates through the senses, we come to
know God through the world, and it is a mistake surely to talk
of anything but intellectual *knowledge*. Our intellect knows God
—or rather, man knows God by means of his intellect, so far as
he can by natural reason alone, not *after* the sensible experience
of the world, but *in* that very experience.

The following passage from the same article prepares the
ground for the chapters which follow:

> Philosophers, I think we do well to remember, are not con-
> fined to the academies, and, when we turn to the problem of
> God we need to think more of the way in which a Christian
> actually talks to an unbeliever. In this, I suggest, we find a clue
> to the proper shape of natural theology. It is, for want of a
> better name, a dialectic of suggestion, an encouragement to
> take another look at the world and *see*. We cannot deny the
> usefulness (at least to us) of a set of stock arguments and
> examples, but we cannot make our conviction that of an un-
> believer until we have shown him where and how to look for
> himself. . . . It is the job of the theist to answer in conjunction
> two main questions: what does *knowing* mean in "knowing
> God", and *what* is it we know in knowing God?

CHAPTER VI

SUPPORT FOR THE SOLUTION IN FRENCH

The "dialectic of suggestion" recommended at the end of the last chapter may sound an unconvincing way of showing that God exists. But you cannot put the knowledge of God into a man's mind as you can put food into his stomach. The evidence is there—in fact, it is everywhere. But when, for one reason or another, it is obscured, there is no automatic way of disclosing it. And we must not jump to the conclusion that the reason is always a discreditable one. Through no fault of his own, a man may be in a state of complete myopia or complete muddle about the whole subject.

GABRIEL MARCEL: ON "RECOLLECTION"

In this chapter we shall take some examples of this dialectic from French Catholic authors who consider that our knowledge of God is of an "intuitive" or, as I prefer to say, "apprehensive" kind, and it is proper that we should begin with M. Gabriel Marcel. He objects to being called an existentialist, but his insistence on personal relationships and on human liberty do link him with other writers to whom the label is attached. He differs from many of them not only in being a Catholic but also in his avoidance (as a rule) of rebarbative language. Yet it must be confessed that he is very elusive when it comes to the point. In his recent essay on God and causality[1] he argues that the "common notion" of causality, charged as

[1] In *De la Connaissance de Dieu*, ed. Jolivet, Bruges, 1958.

it is with mechanical associations, cannot be turned into a metaphysical notion by means of analogy. In place of it, for purposes of natural theology, he suggests the notion of generosity. The category of causality, he says, is essentially a profane one, whereas theological thought should concentrate upon God's transcendence while guarding against the danger of banishing him from the picture altogether. And so we go on, dodging various pitfalls but not, apparently, making much progress.

But it is possible to discover from M. Marcel's writings what his positive views are, and certain guiding principles of his thoughts are in general currency. In particular, he distinguishes between a "problem" and a "mystery". A "mystery" is something which we cannot regard as an "object", as something over against ourselves which we can inspect and judge in a detached way; it is something in which our own being is somehow involved. And if we are to appreciate this, we must perform an act of attention which Marcel calls "recollection".

In his *Metaphysical Journal*[2] he wrote (November 30th, 1930):

> If God is essentially a *thou*, for whom I exist, for whom I matter and who is perhaps only for me in as much as he wills to be, it is easy to understand that he is capable of *not* being for my neighbour. Hence we see why no demonstration of the existence of God is possible. There is no logical transition by which we can mount up to God from a starting-point which is not God. If the ontological [St Anselm's] proof still stands it is because it is established in God at the outset—and in that measure it is superseded as proof.

In *Being and Having*[3] he writes:

> I believe that at least I have begun to see the possibility of examining the very idea of proving the existence of God with regard to the Thomist proofs. It is a fact that they are not universally convincing. How can we explain their partial ineffectiveness? The arguments presuppose that we have already

[2] English Trans., Rockliff, London, 1952, p. 262.
[3] Trans. of *Etre et Avoir*, Dacre Press, London, 1949.

grounded ourselves on God and what they are really doing is to bring to the level of discursive thought an act of a wholly different kind. . . . Thinking of all this, I began to wonder whether my instrument of thought is a reflexive intuition.[4]

And later on in the same book he writes more explicitly:

From this point of view, what becomes of the notion of proving the existence of God? We must obviously subject it to a careful revision. In my view, all proof refers to a certain datum, which is here the belief in God, whether in myself or in another. The proof can only consist in a secondary reflection of the type which I have defined; a reconstructive reflection grafted upon a critical reflection; a reflection which is a recovery, but only in so far as it remains the tributary of what I have called a blindfold intuition.[5]

A careful reading of the last passage will make it clear enough that Marcel is in the "Augustinian" tradition.

AIME FOREST: ON "SPIRITUAL PRESENCE"

Such examples could be multiplied, but I must confine myself to a few representative figures. Let us turn to Prof. Aimé Forest, of Montpellier, who claims to belong to the Thomist tradition but who at the same time has explicitly associated himself with Gabriel Marcel and with Lavelle and Le Senne, to whom we shall turn later. Forest's views are most conveniently to be found, for our purposes, in a book entitled *La Vocation de L'Esprit*, published in 1953; I shall begin with a literal translation of some passages from the penultimate chapter entitled "La Présence spirituelle":

Spiritual activity is a recollection (*reprise de nous–mêmes*) which requires a certain effort. . . . Then we get beyond the mere immediacy of things to find a fuller meaning in all our activities. . . . The revelation which is made to us then is that of a spiritual presence. It can be said that the whole of our inner

[4] P. 98.
[5] P. 14.

effort is directed towards this taking possession and the joy which it promises us. Our experience might be called more a spiritualizing than a spiritual one. It would not be possible if it did not recognize itself as orientated towards an end which attracts it and moves it from within. If we consent to carry out this task by which the life of the spirit is formed in us it produces a profound certainty towards which we are spontaneously led. . . . We must not say that what is present to the mind is only the mind itself.

Forest goes on to say that the experience to which he refers is an experience of *value*. We cannot make this presence a mere object for our enjoyment—it requires our acknowledgement, our assent. And he then speaks of a "presence of the absolute", and of "a discourse which is not equal to the intuition which guides it and towards which it tends". The experience of beauty is then adduced:

[It] always has the character of a contemplative repose. It is an interruption of our ordinary conscious life. Beauty . . . is not only sought for, it is *offered*, and we have the feeling that in this gift it could not be other than it is. . . . So the contemplation of beauty proves to be very close to metaphysical intuition. It makes us pass from the fact of existence to the value of existence. . . . If beauty is accessible to us in a sort of pause, it establishes us in the contemplation of things only by bringing us back to the reality of ourselves. . . . The mind rejoices in beauty because in some sort what it gives us carries the stamp of what we are waiting for, of what was already hinted at. [In the last chapter of the book he is more explicit:] Reflection always makes us grasp at the same time both our limits and our aspirations. We recognize in this experience the idea of the absolute. We cannot deny it, since without it there would be neither thought nor will; nor can we enclose it within the bounds of any nature . . . The idea of the mere possession of the self would have something incomplete about it. With this fresh grasp of all that is implied in our initial enterprise we enter upon religious experience.

"Metaphysical revelation", in short, is the revelation of a "universal presence discovered in each concrete presence".

In conclusion Forest points out that "monastic thought has expressed with a most persuasive clarity and force the idea that the Christian life is the enterprise of discovering the riches of our own souls ... these analyses are the starting-point of modern thought, and they have given our culture its highest principles".... The monastic writers, however, are dealing with the order of grace.

> Philosophy's task is very different. But to perform it we ought not, I think, to abandon the analyses of the spiritual and mystical writers. What we need to do is to realize the characteristics of the new life which Christian teaching shows us in ourselves. Then we can recognize in the Christian order what still belongs to nature and is not abolished, even though it is caught up into this higher order. What is required, then, of philosophical reflection is a discernment within the life of the spirit, especially as analysed by the mystics, of what corresponds there to the aspiration of nature itself. [Thus] religious philosophy aims at discovering the *natural* movement presupposed by the Christian life.

M. Forest's words have introduced us to several fresh aspects of our field of inquiry. They may be at first disconcerting. Vague talk about "value" and about "beauty", we may feel, is surely not enough. And appeals to mysticism and to theology are surely out of place in philosophical analysis. At present I can do little more than ask for patience. These themes will be taken up again by other writers whom we have still to consider, when they may come to seem more securely grounded; and in any case there are many "dialectics of suggestion", and it is not necessary that all of them should appeal to everybody. But the connection of philosophy with theology may be touched on at once. It is quite in order for the Christian philosopher to receive enlightenment from Christianity. In his dialogue with the non-Christian he cannot, indeed, shut out from his mind the truths which his faith has taught him. They teach him the *meaning* of the human predicament; and give him a firmer grasp of the natural basis on which the supernatural life arises. He does not appeal directly to Christian truths, but he must not pretend to be ignorant of them. They guide him to the heart of the matter in his philosophy.

LAVELLE AND LE SENNE: ON "PARTICIPATION IN THE ABSOLUTE"

Louis Lavelle succeeded Bergson at the Collège de France in 1941, and many would consider him second in importance only to Maurice Blondel among the French metaphysicians of his time; this position might be assigned, I think, with at least equal plausibility to his collaborator, René Le Senne. In his inaugural lecture Lavelle described "the demands of French thought" in the following terms:

> To seek the absolute, inside oneself and not outside oneself in the most intimate, personal and profound experience, but an absolute in which we can only participate ... not to reject the intelligence, as we are tempted to do, when its function is to reveal to us the evils from which we are suffering ... not to rely upon emotion, unless it is purified in the life of thought. It is not in avoiding the absolute, but in trying to rediscover it in the events of our lives that we shall give them their true significance, and this will make us capable of appreciating our burden and of accepting it.

Dr École, in a recent book on the metaphysic of being in the philosophy of Louis Lavelle,[6] remarks in his Introduction that "a philosopher who is worthy of the name has never said more than one thing". "What else", he goes on to ask, do we find in Lavelle's chief works save "the same great idea that the being which is my own self is a limited being which has existence and activity only in dependence upon absolute Being, in the creative activity in which it is summoned to participate together with all the other selves from which it is separated by the material world?" Dr École stresses the kinship between Lavelle and Thomism, but he goes too far when he tries to show that the discovery of God, according to Lavelle, is really

[6] Louvain, 1958.

an inferential process. In fact, Lavelle is in complete agreement with Le Senne in this matter.

Le Senne's position can be made clear by a few extracts from his posthumous work *La Découverte de Dieu*.[7] "My philosophy", he there writes, "has three centres: duty, the self and God."[8] "God reveals himself to the individual consciousness by the very nature of the individual consciousness, but this nature is liberty."[9] "That nothing can be understood except by the idea of the infinite is a fresh proof of the existence of God."[10] "Value (*la valeur*) does not come from man, and if it is available for him it is that he may give himself to it . . . it is only this that can sustain him during the trials which he must pass through to attain his proper dignity; this alone can promise him that metaphysical participation in the Absolute which has always been the true goal of philosophy."[11] Later he speaks of a "primary and indivisible value" which lies at the heart of all minds and of all things: "We call it the Absolute when we approach it by the way of knowledge, which demands a concrete universal; we call it Act when it is considered as the moral source of all activity; we call it Being when we rise to it, like the prophetess from Mantinea [in Plato's *Symposium*] by the contemplation of beauty; finally, when religion causes us to love it as the source of charity, its name is God."[12] This may seem a little mysterious, but it is clearly not an inferential process which is here described. And we may conclude with Le Senne's often-quoted remark, which might have seemed out of this context, an appeal to merely subjective "religious experience": "For me the principal proof of God's existence is the joy which I feel in the thought that God exists."[13]

[7] Aubier, Paris, 1955.
[8] P. 21.
[9] P. 23.
[10] P. 10.
[11] P. 107.
[12] P. 112.
[13] P. 18.

MAURICE BLONDEL: ON TRANSCENDENCE
AND IMMANENCE

But the most important of all French Catholic philosophers, at the time of his death in 1949, was Maurice Blondel (it is an astonishing fact that there is no book about him in English). Passages taken from his works would not mean much in isolation, so I shall draw on the findings of his accredited expositor, M. Paul Archambauld, in his *Initiation à la philosophie blondélienne*.[14] The heart of Blondel's work, he tells us, is revealed in the following proposition: "in the very immanence of our spontaneous life an inevitable transcendence is everywhere revealed." This somewhat cryptic pronouncement is then interpreted:

> In us there is something which is more than ourselves, which is separated from us by an abyss, but without which we are inexplicable to ourselves.... This is not a presence which tries to impose itself on us from without and which we might hope to evade, it is a stimulation which is exercised in our furthest depths without which we should not be what we are. It is not a postulate which we find it convenient to put forward; it is an intelligible and enlightening truth by which alone our thought, our being and our activity are made clear to us. How can we fail to recognize in this what man has always called God? *Deus superior summo meo, Deus intimior intimo meo* (St Augustine).
>
> Thus, one may say that, in Blondel's view, there are, strictly speaking, no atheists. There are certainly men who do not know how to discern or to name the unknown God, who already dwells in their hearts, others who fear to canonize idols and superstitions by affirming God, others whom their passions deter from acknowledging what they know at the bottom of their hearts well enough to wish it were not so; but each of these attitudes can reveal a more or less involuntary homage to the Master of our consciences and of our destiny.[15]

Blondel is far from rejecting the traditional "proofs" as useless, but "the classical form of argument makes us conclude

[14] Bloud et Gay, Paris, 1941.
[15] Pp. 79, 80.

from the contingent to the necessary: M. Blondel seeks to show the necessary as present in the contingent itself".[16] It should be added that Blondel rejects the word "intuition" in this connection. No one has insisted more strongly on the combination of certainty and obscurity which characterizes our knowledge of God.[17]

No doubt this has become monotonous. But the passages which I have been quoting, although they all illustrate what is fundamentally the same thesis, are not simply repetitions of one another. They have been chosen so as to bring out the manysidedness of the "metaphysical experience" as well as to demonstrate the impressive backing which this point of view can claim. A few more such passages are still required to show that it is shared by theologians of the highest standing as well as by philosophers.

FR DE LUBAC: ON THE RECOGNITION OF GOD

The obvious first choice for the purpose is Fr Henri de Lubac's *Sur les Chemins de Dieu*, published in English translation under the title of *The Discovery of God*.[18] The history of this work is significant. In 1945 Fr de Lubac produced a little book on our knowledge of God which met with considerable criticism. It seemed to his critics that he was turning his back on scholasticism in general and Thomism in particular and taking up dangerous modern philosophies of an "ontologist" kind, philosophies, that is, which claim an *immediate* intuition of God. *Sur les Chemins de Dieu* was Fr de Lubac's answer to his critics. All the key-passages of the original work are still found in this second, much longer, book. He has not found it necessary to withdraw anything of importance which he had said, despite the fact that the Encyclical *Humani Generis*, in 1950, had put ecclesiastical censors on their guard

---

[16] P. 82.

[17] Cf. in particular *L'Etre et les Etres*, Alcan, Paris, 1935, Excursus 18.

[18] Darton, Longman and Todd, London, 1960.

against those tendencies which his original work had been supposed to exhibit. In the circumstances the reappearance of these passages with the *Imprimatur* is a peculiarly effective guarantee of their orthodox character, although a certain nervousness is still to be detected in the reviews of the translation by theologians, in England and Ireland, of the more conventional sort. The book is discursive and meditative—not a philosophical or theological treatise, but an anthology of Christian writings, ancient, medieval and modern, on the discovery of God, and a record of the author's own reflections on the fundamental religious problem of our time.

In the introductory section Fr de Lubac writes:

> God reveals himself to man by imprinting his image upon him. That divine operation constitutes the very centre of man. That is why, strictly speaking, no other revelation is absolutely necessary; that natural revelation suffices, quite apart from any supernatural revelation. But in order to avoid exaggeration, let us say that it suffices in principle. Sin has not entirely extinguished it.[19] [He concludes the section with a reference to St Augustine:] "Know yourself by knowing your God. Begin, as far as possible for a mortal, to contemplate his Face in recollection."[20]

It was at first my impression that, in this book, Fr de Lubac was adopting, or at least occasionally countenancing, the position of Fr Jolivet and others that our knowledge of God involves an implicit syllogism. But a passage from the second chapter, "The Affirmation of God", shows his mind clearly enough: after referring to a remark of Fr Scheuer's ("God being without principle cannot be affirmed by a principle distinct from himself"), Fr de Lubac continues:

> That does not mean that reasoning—according to logical principles—in order to prove the existence of God is superfluous, but that the thought, which is our affirmation of God, is not the

[19] P. 16.
[20] P. 17. It is possible that Fr de Lubac goes too far in interpreting St Thomas and the Thomists in an Augustinian sense, but this need not worry us.

conclusion of an argument. The thought which reasons comes
before the reasoning. And if reasoning must perforce intervene,
that is in order to show us what thought consists in or what it
implies ... the existence of God is not a truth among other
truths, a particular truth dependent *in itself* upon another,
greater truth, or a more comprehensive and fundamental truth
of which it is, in some sort, one of several possible applications.
In other words, the Being of God is not a particular Being with
its place among others, at the beginning of, or within, a series.
God is not the first link in the chain of being. . . . God is the
reality which envelops, dominates and measures our thought,
and not the reverse. He is the reality which makes our thought
at once so great and sure of itself, so absolute in its judgements
and so necessarily obedient.[21]

Again this is St Augustine's proof. And the intervention of
reason takes the form of showing us that, if we deny the
"proof", we fall into a contradiction, not, as Fr de Lubac has
pointed out earlier, "a particular logic contradiction—which is
always possible, but a total, vital, spiritual contradiction, a
contradiction in the being who thinks, a sin by the spirit
against the spirit".[22]

The chapter on "The Proof of God" emphasizes that the
principle common to all the proofs cannot be invalidated
"because it forms part of the substance of the mind".[23]
Fr de Lubac's various dicta about the "proof" are not always
formally consistent, and the reviewer in *The Times Literary
Supplement* availed himself of this fact in order to dismiss the
book. We are told at one point that "the apparatus of the
proofs is surely nothing but a vast *removens prohibens*—a
clearing away of obstacles",[24] yet he often speaks of them as
if they could provide us, in their own right, with a conclusion
of a kind, a "notional" rather than a "real" conclusion, to use
Newman's language, and he is sometimes led to speak of them
as "justifying" the conclusion. This is the result of his tendency

[21] Pp. 41–2.
[22] P. 40.
[23] P. 66.
[24] P. 77.

to claim a general agreement in the matter among Christian
thinkers which does not exist. But what he really means is
perfectly clear: "All men know God 'naturally', but they do
not always recognize him ... when I come to know God as the
one who will make me happy, I realize at the same time that
God is identified with the beatitude which I knew by desiring
it, but which I placed, at first, among objects which deceived
me; or rather I can now identify my beatitude with him. That
is certainly recognition."[25]

The chapter on "The Knowledge of God" confirms this
verdict: "Being created by the Word, everything which comes
from him is a word and speaks of him. It is for me to attend
and to answer—but the initiative is not mine. By that very
fact, such knowledge of God the creator, though always
mediated, is not entirely indirect. To borrow a word from
St Augustine, one might call it *contuitio*."[26] And Fr de Lubac,
too, illustrates this by referring to moral obligation: "If God
is already known in some way in our knowledge of duty (even
by those who think themselves unable to see him and call
themselves atheists), it may be said that God is found and
possessed in some way in the fulfilment of duty. However, that
can be said only upon one condition ... duty must be regarded
not as a purely formal law in the Kantian sense, but as the
requirement of the Good."[27] Finally, the distinction between
natural and supernatural knowledge is emphasized: "Then, to
our astonishment, the Gift of God intervenes. It is the second
gift, for the first is the gift of mind itself, of the affirmation....
It is as though a new dimension had been introduced. By
allowing us to participate in the Life of God himself, the life
of charity furnishes our idea of God with a spiritual content."[28]

[25] Pp. 78–80.
[26] Pp. 94–5.
[27] P. 103.
[28] Pp. 110–11.

FR BOUYER: ON THE MEANING OF LOVE

Our last witness is perhaps the best known of living French theologians in the English-speaking countries, Fr Louis Bouyer; he is, moreover, a theologian of distinctly "conservative" tendencies, the last person to take up with a mere fashion in theology or with anything that savours of an attack on genuinely traditional positions. In his *L'Initiation Chrétienne* he writes as follows:

What is true in the case of the discovery of mind or spirit in general is also true in the case of the discovery of God. Really, the discovery of God is itself only a higher degree, a final extension, of the discovery of spirit. It could be said that, as we discover together our body and the physical world in which it is immersed, so we discover together spirit in ourselves and in God. It has been suggested that the etymology of the word religion is connected with this fundamental discovery of the bond between ourselves and God, a closer bond than that between our body and the world, although a very different one.

In the discovery of God by man, then, we start from a deeply-rooted, pre-existing intuition. Subsequent experience may sometimes tend to obscure or cloud it, but persevering thought will find it again enriched and illuminated. However, here even more than in the case of the discovery of spirit, the activity of the reasoning intelligence alone cannot be certain of arriving at the goal if it is isolated from human experience as a whole. In particular, the intelligence will be fatally crippled in its climb, and stop prematurely in half-discoveries, or even sheer sophistries, if the intellectual search is not accompanied by the normal development of that moral experience in which the soul recovers possession of itself in its deepest and highest manifestations.

Moral experience, as we have said, cannot be reduced simply to the experience of duty or obligation, which is simultaneously higher, transcendent and inward. It also includes the experience of our relationships with others, capable as they are of evolving into the purest and richest forms of friendship or love. Religious experience could be described as what moral experience becomes when its various forms are unified at the top. In the religious experience, in fact, the mysterious experience of moral obligation is illuminated by the discovery of the quite special relationship in which we find ourselves with someone: someone who is capable of creating an incomparable love in us, someone who wishes to form with us a friendship of which all others are only an image or sketch, someone above all who loves us before we have ever thought of him, who loves us with a love the discovery of which will completely transfigure for us the whole meaning of the word "love".

The experience which we have just described is the highest peak to which the discovery of God will bring us. But, once again, this experience is, as it were, foreshadowed and prefigured by an elementary, fundamental experience. For it is not enough to say that we find religion at the basis of all human civilizations and cultures. It would be truer to say that religion appears, as primitive setting and impulse, behind every activity in the world and every view of the world elaborated by man.

[29] English trans., *Christian Initiation*, Burns & Oates, London, 1960, pp. 21–3.

CHAPTER VII

THE APPREHENSION
OF GOD

It is time to gather up the strands. At present they may still seem scattered and insubstantial. In fact they make up something quite solid, like strands of a rope. The evidence of God's existence is there to be looked for, but it is not easy to teach people *how* to look. And one reason for this is that, in all probability, they have already looked and seen without realizing what it was that they were doing. We must also face the possibility that they have looked and seen and then deliberately looked away; but this is a conclusion which should be reached only after prolonged inquiry, and in any case it is probably better not to mention it but instead to go on providing opportunities.

THE MORAL EVIDENCE AND JUDGEMENTS OF VALUE

For most people the most accessible of the facts with which we have to deal is the fact of moral obligation, and it will therefore be best to begin with it. And the most important thing which has to be made clear about it is that we are here concerned, fundamentally, not with obligations to do this or that but with the fact of obligation in general, the fact that we are called upon to do *something*, that we are not morally free to be quite inactive, to leave our capacities wholly undeveloped. Of course, it will be said, no normal person wants to do that—

it is too boring; there is no need to bring in the notion of *duty*. There is, though—it may not be much to the fore in a person's mind, and it may manifest itself only in a dim sort of way and only when particular obligations (to one's family, for example) obtrude themselves; but a recognition that one is not simply one's own master can be detected as a *leitmotiv* in human history. The fact that people have differed, and still differ, so much about what their obligations actually are, is thus irrelevant. Morality, duty, is not disqualified as a fact of human history because moral codes have varied so widely and have even contradicted one another in important matters.

Bradley put the point succinctly in *Ethical Studies*, when he spoke of "an end which I am to make real" and added that "morality, if not equivalent to, is at all events included in this making real of myself".[1] It must be emphasized that there is no question of an *explicit* recognition of this in all cases. The claim is that this fundamental deliverance of the conscience shows itself regularly in operation. When attention is drawn to it, it cannot be denied by anyone who has a modicum of education. But "education" here means more than the ability to read and write and to make money. It implies that a certain natural development has already taken place, that a certain innocent wonder has not been stifled at birth, that a certain interest in oneself and one's surroundings has not been atrophied from the start by a pervasive materialism or by a life-long struggle for physical necessities. Some sort of education, in the sense which I am indicating, may be the indispensable preliminary to any dialogue about God's existence. And in any case it remains open to anyone to maintain that the sense of duty is simply the result of heredity and environment; he will not deny the facts, but he will deny that they have any metaphysical significance. He cannot produce proof of this; but the metaphysician cannot prove that he is wrong except by persuading him to consider more attentively the deliverance of his own conscience. Apart from this the most that can be done is to show why the theory is unplausible. And

[1] P. 84, 2nd edn, Oxford University Press, 1927.

even to see that it is unplausible involves a judgement of *value*.

Let us see how such a dialogue develops in a typical case. A young man, let us say (I am recalling an incident in my own experience), has occasion to call upon a priest because he wants to marry a Catholic. He declares himself entirely without religion or interest in religion. The facts of the moral life are adduced as pointing in the direction of religion. The young man rejects them. In the end he is asked whether he feels no obligation to the girl, whether his attitude to her is a purely self-regarding one, whether she is not for him a person with rights to be respected, someone to be valued for what she is, whether his love for her is really compatible with the exclusively "scientific" account which he claims to give of all human experience. If he knows his business as a "positivist" and is determined to give nothing away, he may simply dismiss all these considerations. If he is intelligent he may realize that any admission of metaphysical realities puts him on a slippery slope which ends in religion. So he may dig himself in. Any other such approach may be staved off in just the same way. If a man is not willing to recognize that there are *values* in life which cannot be explained away by the joint efforts of anthropologists, psycho-analysts, "linguistic" philosophers and so forth, then there can be no advance. It is no use to say to him that the greater cannot be produced by the lesser because he is not willing to allow the distinction between greater and lesser, unless it is merely the distinction between the more and the less complicated. Why should it not be simply the way of the world that things should complicate themselves? If you say that any sort of development requires an explanation (moving over to the consideration of causality in general) he may again reply that things just happen to behave as they do, that it is pointless to ask questions to which there can be no answer.

But such a dialogue, even if it seems to end nowhere, may not have been useless. A seed of disquiet may have been planted. At least the issues have been plainly presented, and the implications of the positivist standpoint may begin to seem extravagant. It may be gradually borne in upon a man that our culture has been built up by judgements of value, that the acknowledged leaders of thought in past ages, the philosophers as well as the artists and the saints, are very difficult to account for in the mass from the positivist standpoint. Can we avoid passing judgements of value when we consider such men? Can we say that the man whom Arnold Toynbee has called *homo mechanicus neobarbarus* is really "normal" or "standard" man and that the rest are misguided fools? And even if we do, are we not passing a judgement of value by doing so?

It can be said in reply that to take a way of life as a "normal" one means only to decide that it seems likely to bring more happiness than any other to the human race as a whole. It is simply a statement of the facts. The mere seeking of pleasure and the avoidance of pain require no explanation; there is nothing metaphysical about the value which we attach to them. Call it, if you like, a judgement of value; but you can make nothing of it. And again, if anyone decides to maintain that position, logic cannot force him out of it. But that seems to be the natural point of transition to a rather different approach.

THE VALUE OF TRUTH

Let us grant, for the sake of argument, that there is nothing at stake save a knowledge of the facts about human happiness, how it is best gained and how preserved. Let us further assume, again for the sake of argument, that there could be a science of human happiness for *homo mechanicus neobarbarus*, a formula which would work. We may now ask: what is the importance, for the individual, of knowing these facts, of finding the formula? Is it simply that he may apply it for his own private purposes? Most people would be willing to allow that the happiness of others does concern them, but, as we have seen, if they take up a positivist stand, they will want to explain it in self-regarding terms—the knowledge that other people are miserable naturally has a depressing effect on us, or there happens to be a certain sympathy among men which makes the happiness of others necessary to us; we are just made like that. But the question can be pressed: is that the only importance of knowing facts apart from the use to which you put them? Isn't there something sacred about facts to the scientists? And isn't the word "sacred", when you come to think of it, an appropriate one?

That needs to be made explicit. The question which is now being asked comes to this: doesn't it *matter* that you should know the truth about the business in hand, the formula for human happiness or whatever else it may be? Hasn't it an importance because it is the truth? Isn't there a demand for truth in the human mind? Isn't there a *duty* to know the truth or at least avoid self-deception? And still it may be said that we just happen to be made like that, that it has no far-reaching implications. Yet it is surely at this point that the positivist position should seem most obviously untenable. Once the question of truth is seriously entertained, it is hard to see how it can be honestly dismissed, although its implications may be at first quite obscure. And the alternative to positivism, in the twentieth century, is not any form of non-theist idealism; by and large, the evolving Absolute or Culture or Beauty or Moral Perfection in the abstract have ceased to seem the final goal of man and a sufficient motive for his endeavours—in so far as people think on these lines at all, these expressions have come to seem (as indeed they are) hopelessly vague and unsatisfying, aspirations which float about between earth and heaven, enigmatic and without foundation. That seems to be true as a generalization; it is at least typical of twentieth-century man. And that is why I shall not spend time in this book refuting pantheism or nineteenth-century liberalism and romanticism.

The topic of obligation thus broadens into the general topic of the human situation, of the fact that we have minds and souls as well as bodies. Duty is indeed simply the most obvious aspect of that situation for most people, but until it has been seen in its context its significance will not be properly appreciated. In the same way the significance of the mind or soul will not be properly appreciated if the consciousness of obligation and the making of value-judgements are not recognized as essential features of it. Truth-judgements and value-judgements are bound up with one another. To recognize that something is true is not merely to decide that you can rely on your information, that you can make something work. It is to find something from which there is no *legitimate* escape; we may succeed in putting it out of our minds, if we happen to dislike it, but we can hardly fail to be aware, at some time in our lives at least, that in such a case we are doing a sort of violence to ourselves. At this point we can see that something is meant, after all, by speaking of our "true" selves. We can recognize, moreover, that any other mind which may exist, if it does not reach a conclusion to which we have certainly come, *ought* to reach it. Truth, the rock-bottom which we can touch if we try, is something over against all of us. There is a standard for all minds, and it should come to seem more and more unplausible that this should be just another fact which we can record dispassionately and impersonally.

Why, let us ask again, should we desire the truth? What value can there be in finding things out if they seem not to serve any practical purpose? Why not spend all the time in day-dreaming, if you enjoy it and have the opportunity? Perhaps because people would make fun of you. But doesn't the question of self-respect arise? And what is there about ourselves which we should respect? There does seem to be something about us which makes this claim. If for some mysterious reason we claim our own respect, what about other people and other things? Don't they also claim it? This is perhaps the way in which the notion of value may be made more explicit, so that the question of a *source of values* becomes more urgent. Why, then, should it seem so important that men should see things as they are? Why should some things at least seem to have a value for their own sakes? They make a claim upon us, but, when we look into it, there seems at first to be no justification for their claims; they are just *things*. We are forced behind them to account for their value. Taken by themselves, they are not valuable, yet value is present to them. There is only one satisfying account of this matter: that they are derived values, that the value which they have is not their own. This is paradoxical, but it makes sense. It means that they are without value, taken by themselves, precisely because they do not exist by themselves. They owe what they are to God. They are "reflections" of God. We are brought back to the topic mentioned in previous chapters of the relationship which is found between creatures and God when once God's existence has been discovered. So what we are doing here is to illustrate the apprehension of God by some attempt to describe its effects. If the effects are recognized, it may be allowed that they are effects of this apprehension. This is a "monstration", not a "demonstration", that we have knowledge of God.

Such a "monstration" can hardly avoid going round and round, in the hope, as Plato put it, that the light may at some point break through. For the moment we must pursue the subject of "reflection" a little further. What we seem to have been saying is that it is really God whom we value when we seem to be valuing his creatures. It is *because* they are "reflections" of God that they have value. But this does not mean *merely* that we see through them to him or find him acting in them. It means also that his creatures, although always deriving from him, brought into being by him, are not without an intelligible relation to him. We find in them not only God's activity but (in a roundabout way) something about God's nature. We discover that creatures are "signs" of God, a showing forth of qualities which are aspects of his nature. God is absolute simplicity and absolute richness at the same time. His creatures display in a limited, fragmented, form this absolute richness. In God they are unlimited and are identified, fused, with one another. This may seem unintelligible, but it is the result which has been reached with a startling unanimity by the greatest religious minds. God's creatures have values of their own by "representing" God in their own special ways, showing us that something in God's absolute richness (although here words are only "pointers") corresponds to each of them. This had to be said if we were not to run away from a difficulty.

THE EVIDENCE OF OUR SPIRITUAL POWERS

But the difficulty results from the detection of God's activity; it is not something which must be overcome as a preliminary. The detection itself occurs, fundamentally, in the inner life. Even if our bent is to look outwards to the general scene, to the human situation viewed abstractly, we must bring with us (although we may hardly be aware of it) some hint of the essential clue. Knowledge of the self and knowledge of the world are interdependent. But the source of our metaphysical discoveries seems to be the self. Thus when we consider the material world in itself and in isolation, we shall find in it no convincing" argument from design", or any rate no convincing argument for the Infinite. We could not satisfy ourselves that it must have a purpose if we had no inkling that there is a purpose for ourselves. We have knowledge of God, then, in that his designs upon us are, in a measure, manifested. It is present to us as drawing us to him. But this is not an appeal to human aspirations in contradistinction to an appeal to intellectual or metaphysical experience, just as Pascal's "knowledge of the heart" is not an appeal simply to the affections but to that "centre" of the soul where intellect and will are interwoven. There is a real contact of the mind with God, but it is the beginning of a dynamic process and is experienced as such.

It will be useful for us at this point to consider rather more closely how the "inner life" should be understood in the present context. A scientist absorbed in his investigations clearly enjoys a very vigorous "inner life" in one sense. His mind is hard at work; he calculates, analyses, reflects, constructs hypotheses— but he has no interest, as a scientist, in personal reactions. And so scientists when they turn to philosophy are often tempted to produce accounts which, in effect, abolish the observer altogether. We may be inclined to say that thinking ought to be an impersonal affair, but here we must make distinctions. Philosophical thought, although it must be purely objective— that is purely receptive and unprejudiced, open to reality without reserves or "wishful thinking"—is the thought of a person in a situation. A man must face up to himself and his situation as well as to everything else; everything must be accounted for, if he is to be purely objective. But the "inner life" in the sense with which we are concerned means more than this. It refers also to that development of the personality which occurs as the *reaction* to this purely objective contemplation of our world and of ourselves. Using our minds as they ought to be used gives us an insight into the true nature of the mind itself. We become aware of its potentialities—we become aware, in other words, of God's activity in it. (For some people this is most obviously the case in the contemplation of great works of art.) The "inner life", then, for our purposes, is not an affair of introspection in the ordinary sense. It is in surrendering our minds to reality, in becoming absorbed in it, that we discover ourselves.

The recognition of this fundamental paradox is not brought about, in the first place, by turning in upon ourselves. But, if it is to be fruitful, a certain concentration on it must follow. "Whosoever will save his life shall lose it, and whosoever will lose his life shall save it"—A. E. Housman called this "the most important truth which has ever been uttered, and the greatest discovery ever made in the moral world";[2] yet he wrote his poems as an atheist, and called himself an agnostic. It may be merely a muddle; or it may be that he had given up the attempt to attend to God, or, in the language of Christians, to pray.

When we decide to take ourselves seriously, to treat the problem of the human mind as a serious problem, when we recognize this as a *duty*, we are already, I submit, turning to God, although we may have only a suspicion, as yet, that it is God to whom we are turning, or we may even fail to recognize that religion comes into it at all. To take the problem seriously is to have already glimpsed the answer to it. What is proposed to us is a value-judgement about the mind itself. If we can no longer treat it as an epiphenomenon—as the mere froth, as

[2] *The Name and Nature of Poetry*, Cambridge University Press, 1933, p. 36.

it were, which forms on the beer (the beer in this case being blind energies)—there seems no escaping the conclusion that we are of more importance than the other mindless occupants of our planet. And if once we begin to pass serious value-judgements, as we have seen, we are in position for apprehending the source of values. Indeed, in so far as these judgements are really serious, we are already apprehending, although we are not yet certain.

FACING THE ALTERNATIVE—THE ABSURD

Now we may draw back, deterred by God's apparent absence in the world outside us and by an apparent threat to our independence—we still suspect that our inner experience is illusory. What settles the matter is perhaps most often a good look at the alternative. The alternative is to conclude that there is no purpose in human life and in the world around us, to call our experience *absurd*. Everything is then absurd, and it is the great merit of Jean Paul Sartre to have made this so clear for us. We must recognize this, he tells us, or we shall be in "bad faith". But how can we be in "bad faith" if there is no "good faith"? Sartre, it might seem, is attacking not the true God, but a god made in man's image or the "god of this world" against whom Blake waged an unceasing war ("The lost traveller's dream under the hill"). And if this is so, he is agreeing with Blake that we must have something genuine to worship:

> If the Sun and Moon should doubt
> They'd immediately Go out.

It is a Christian truth (the most baffling perhaps of all truths) that it is possible to reject God absolutely, to turn away from him in full consciousness of what we are doing. We have to keep that possibility in mind. But it presupposes a knowledge of God. For the philosopher of religion, who wants to promote that knowledge, it is indifference which is the real enemy.

Taking a good look at the alternative is a method of un-earthing the apprehension of God which can be applied in various ways. Can we write off the knowledge of God which people claim to have as a figment of the imagination? For, if it is not genuine, that is what it must be. It may be suggested that religion is just a dream, an escape from the harsher reali-ties of life, originally based upon credulity and self-deceptions, capable of imposing itself, as it gains momentum, upon better-developed minds, yet always fundamentally "pie in the sky". But really this will not do. Even a slight acquaintance with the history of religion should show that there is more in it than just a desire for happiness, for a "good time". There is in it the desire for spiritual perfection, and if this desire does not result from a knowledge of God it is by no means obvious how we are to account for it. Certainly the presence of a desire does not prove in all cases that there must be an existing object capable of fulfilling it (it is unsound to base an apologetic argument on this, considered as a general or abstract prin-ciple). But there are some desires which require to be explained and which, it seems, can be explained only by the attraction of such an object. In other words, how could we have invented for ourselves this standard of perfection? This is not the same as saying that we cannot use the idea of justice, for ex-ample, without involving ourselves in metaphysical considera-tions. We can give a perfectly satisfactory account of what we mean by justice in terms of human behaviour, confining our-selves to "empirical" facts which are plain enough to every-body. What we have to account for here may be summed up as the idea of perfect love. Could it be only an "idea"? We do not, in fact, find it realized in our relations with other people; we may think that we do for a time, but as our experience grows we find that there is always a barrier which we cannot pass. For we never completely *know* one another. Perfect love is not merely the love which we have for one another with all the little rifts closed up and the little misunderstandings ironed out. It is something of which, in these relationships, we are essentially incapable. Yet we know, somehow and in some measure, what it is.

We found that the upshot of St Anselm's argument was to put before us considerations of just this kind. If we acknowledge that it does mean something to speak of a being "than which there can be nothing greater", then we have an "idea" of God, and we cannot have produced it out of our own resources. The "idea" of the infinite, if it has a positive character, cannot have been generated by the finite. If we still view it as only an "idea", then it is not yet for us an apprehension but only a suspicion of God. Suspicion may turn into conviction if we ask ourselves seriously and persistently whether we could have invented such an "idea".

The question is, in the end: *Has* the "idea" of God a positive character? Has it a content? If we can say "yes", then we have, presumably, knowledge of God. If we can honestly say "no", we must have fallen into some confusion. Possibly we have misconceived the question, supposing that an idea, if it has a content, must be describable. But God, if he exists, is necessarily indescribable. It is the hall-mark of a genuine knowledge of God that it cannot be dissected and then offered for inspection to somebody who professes ignorance of it. We can only put him in the way of gaining it. The Infinite is indescribable precisely because it is *absolutely* positive, and cannot therefore be conceived as finite things can be conceived by a process of comparison and contrast with other finite things. But since creatures in fact stand to God in an "analogical" relationship, we may try to exhibit them in that relationship, and so to provoke the "apprehension" or the acknowledgement of it. That, as we saw, was the true function of the Five Ways according to many modern writers, Catholic and non-Catholic. And that is the purpose of this chapter.

THE EVIDENCE AS A UNITY IN DIVERSITY

Throughout it is a single experience to which we are pointing, an experience which reflects its object in that it is at the same time rich and simple. The object is unlike any other object, so that it can be misleading to call it an object, and the experience is unlike any other experience, so that it can be misleading to call it an experience. It is an awareness which underlies all that we should normally call experience. It is rich because it is an awareness of the human situation in its totality; and by the same token it is simple. It can take many forms. It shows us ourselves and the world in which we live as *dependent*, and a closer attention to it reveals in time that what we are aware of is in fact the active presence of the Infinite. Usually a particular form will predominate in particular cases. But the predominant form will merge with, or at least will not exclude, other forms. It may be that the *desire* for the Infinite will be the predominant form. This has been called a Sixth Way of proving God's existence, that is, it is a distinct way in having a distinct starting-point; but it is not until it reveals an apprehension of God (how can we desire what we know nothing about?) that it makes sense. And then it should enlighten and be enlightened by the other aspects of our experience, the facts of the moral and spiritual life, the whole life of the human soul.

If one wishes to point to a predominant form it is probably best to choose that form which predominates in one's own experience—it may not be so striking for others, but at least one may hope to be a little clearer about it than about other forms. So I shall conclude by mentioning those considerations which, for me, exhibit the apprehension of God with peculiar force.

They have emerged, more or less, already. It will be recalled that a claim to know the truth, according to Mr Hartland-Swann, is only a claim to have discovered the "dominant decision" about the matter in hand, the decision which has been reached by a general agreement on the part of those qualified to judge. Now this, I have argued, is altogether unsatisfactory. When we claim to know things as they really are, we mean more than this. We mean that things are what they are whether we know them or not; discovering the truth about

them is to discover *them*. To say that something is true is to
say not only that we discover it but that it *is*. "It *is*" is implied
by, but means something more than, "I know it". It will not
do to say that "existence" stands for nothing in itself—that it
is merely a word which we use about the things which we
know and refers only to the fact that they are known by us.
And "existence" does not describe or refer to some particular
characteristic of these things. It applies to them in their
entirety, and to each of them in the same way. We know that
it applies not only to the things which in fact we know but to
whatever things we do not know. "Existence" is now seen to
involve an *absoluteness*.[3] Yet the things which we know do not
possess, of themselves and in themselves, absoluteness. At this
point it becomes clear, for me, that we are in fact looking
beyond "things" when we say, with full awareness of all these
facts, that they *are*. Moreover, if "existence" applies to all of
them in the same way,[4] and if it refers to them in their entirety,
it cannot be a common character which they all share—for
that would abolish their differences. It can only refer to the
relation in which they stand to a common *source*.

Things, then, are what they are because *God* knows them.
Scientia Dei causa rerum.[5] They have absoluteness in that they
"reflect" him. That is what makes them intelligible. They are
derived realities. For (to repeat) it is not meaningless to say
that they are; it does not mean just that they stand in a relation
to ourselves; it cannot refer only to some part of them—what
is left to us but to pass beyond them, to say that to "exist"
means "to be a *creature*"? The alternative is the Sartrian doctrine of the absurd: if there is no "Father of lights", there is

[3] The same contention is made, in terms of "activity", by Dom Mark
Pontifex in the second chapter of his contribution to this series, *Providence and Freedom*.
[4] The Thomist thesis about existence is that it is an analogous notion.
It seems clear to me that our use of the word implies a real *sameness*
of some kind in all that is said to exist.
[5] The knowledge of God is the cause of things (St Thomas). Berkeley
had insight into this when he concluded that there can be nothing
which is not known by *some* mind, that there must be a creative mind
which knows all things.

no unity, no intelligibility, in the world; there is no fixed foundation on which our minds can rest. But we can be certain that this is not the case. The fact that we can be certain of anything can show us this. For when we are *certain*, we can realize that our minds are at work as they are *meant* to be at work—if we have grasped something with our minds (if only that the conclusion of a syllogism really *is* a conclusion), if we say that it is *true*, we can realize that we have pierced to the heart of things, that we belong to a world of intelligibles, a world which has a meaning. If we are doing what we are *meant* to do, we are in touch with and enlightened by, the creative mind. That is why the words of the fourth psalm have a special appeal for Augustinians: *Signatum est super nos lumen vultus tui, Domine: dedisti lætitiam in corde meo.*

CHAPTER VIII

OBJECTIONS

Three groups of objections remain to be considered. The first group would be put forward by theists who discount or distrust the sort of knowledge which was the subject of the last chapter. The answers to most objections of that kind have already emerged in the course of the book, but it seems necessary to set them out clearly in summary form. The objections in the second group are directed against the view that the absoluteness of moral obligation has a religious character; agnostics may object that they are clear about the obligatoriness of certain actions and equally clear that they do not believe in God; and many modern philosophers, including certain theists, will say that ethics is autonomous—that is, it must not be based on (or even, according to some, in any way connected with) metaphysics, if we are not to fall into a logical confusion. The third group of objections concerns the problem of evil. It is probably the existence of evil more than anything else which makes people call themselves unbelievers. A book in this series has been entirely devoted to the problem, but it treats it almost exclusively from a theological (dogmatic) point of view. Another book in this series, to which reference has already been made and with which the present writer is in fundamental agreement, Dom Mark Pontifex's *Providence and Freedom*, does deal with the philosophical issues, and the principles there laid down will be considered here in the light of our earlier chapters. The discussion will be, of necessity, extremely brief (many subsidiary questions will not be touched on at all), but it will go to the heart of the matter.

DOES THE SOLUTION MAKE CLAIMS WHICH ARE EXCESSIVE?

Some theists will no doubt continue to say that the natural knowledge of God claimed in the last chapter is a knowledge which is not in fact available for us. They might begin by observing that our account of it, as it proceeded, drew more and more upon specifically religious ideas, and that the natural knowledge of God can provide us only with the haziest idea of a power behind the scenes. In reply we should remind them of our contention that grace must be accepted freely but that the offer of grace is made necessarily—for all men are summoned, somehow and at some time, to the acceptance of God as their end; so when the offer of grace is made, it may be accepted or rejected—we are still in the natural order, for we are not yet in the state of grace, but at that moment we must know in some sort who God is if we are to make our choice. It seemed reasonable to conclude that the first genuine moral choice (involving the genuine "ought") is at the same time this offer of grace, that the reception of grace follows upon the right choice. If the thesis seems extravagant in this form, it can be put more generally as follows: if all men are to be judged by God, many of them must be judged on the basis of moral choices which have nothing to do with revelation or even with what we ordinarily mean by religion; those who "do what is in them", even if imperfectly, cannot be rejected by God, and there are, no doubt, vast numbers of such people who have no explicit religious creed. But if there is material for judgement in these choices it must be that they are, at bottom, directed Godwards, and that the moral consciousness involves an awareness of God, although it may not be recognized as such. We shall consider later the special difficulties which modern philosophers feel about this binding-up of ethics with metaphysics.

The language which was used in the last chapter about our knowledge of God was indeed making explicit what is only implicit in the earliest stages of this knowledge. But it should

mean something even to those who have not yet passed beyond
these stages. For knowledge of God always carries with it the
note of "recognition". Even revealed knowledge seems to wake
an answering echo in our minds. And the natural knowledge
of God never comes to us as something for which we were
wholly unprepared. The fact seems to be that the presence of
God works upon our minds at so early a stage and in so
obscure a way that we do not at first *advert* to it at all. When
we begin to do so, we can realize that it *has* been present in
this obscure form. Moreover in any actual dialogue about
God's existence we have to remember that our interlocutor,
despite his professions of agnosticism, may very well possess
in fact far more than a minimum awareness of God. If he is an
earnest seeker after truth, this will be presumably the case.
Again there may be a fund of knowledge *about* Christianity
and the Christian God to which we may appeal when we are
talking to "post-Christians" in the hope that a mere "notion"
may become in time an accepted reality. The natural knowledge of God, then, does not exist in a vacuum or as a per-
manent condition (it is a stage rather than a state), and when
we speak of it we must supply it with a context.

THE CHARGE OF ONTOLOGISM

But the objection that an excessive claim is being made will
be pressed with greater urgency from quite a different point of
view. Despite all that I have said it will be, no doubt, reaffirmed
that the "apprehension" of God must be an "intuition" of God,
and that to claim an intuition of God is to fall into the philosophical error of Ontologism which has been condemned by
the Church. It is true, as we have seen, that to claim an
immediate intuition of God is contrary to Catholic teaching,
but I have maintained that we have an "apprehension" of
God which, although it has a character of directness, is nevertheless mediate. We know our own minds mediately in the
sense that it is only in this or that of their activities that we
know them. We know God mediately in the sense that it is

(primarily, at least) only in his activity upon the mind that we know him. Our knowledge of God is thus doubly mediate. God's creatures are always in the foreground of our thought. We apprehend him only "out of the corner of our eye". And so we might go on, piling metaphor on metaphor in the attempt to describe a form of knowledge which is, from the nature of the case, unique. If we say that it is altogether indirect, then, so I have argued, we can give no intelligible account of it at all. But it is there, and we must therefore use the word "direct" about it.

It has become firmly fixed in the minds of most Catholic thinkers that there can be nothing "direct" in our knowledge of God on this earth, for that is reserved entirely for heaven. To know God directly is to know him face to face. It is all or nothing. But it is commonly allowed that there are degrees of the Beatific Vision. Why should there not be for us here a "direct" knowledge of God in very different conditions but still justifying the language of greater and less? Why should there not be a very "distant" knowledge of God which can become rather less "distant"? It may seem odd that there should be a contact of the mind with God which is so unsatisfying, so patently incomplete. But it is not clear what good reason we have for calling it odd. Anyhow, it appears to be the fact.

Before leaving this subject we should refer once more to Dr Hawkins' treatment of it in *The New Outline of Modern Knowledge*.[1] He laid it down that "it is scarcely possible to doubt that knowledge must be either immediate or mediate, i.e. inferential", but we have seen that a good many people have succeeded in doubting whether "mediate" and "inferential" do mean the same thing. He goes on to speak of "a bold attempt to represent the awareness of God as the result of an analysis of the datum of experience", and quotes me as maintaining that "we do not understand what the being of a finite thing means until we have seen that it involves a relationship to pure or infinite being". His comment on this is that

[1] *Op. cit.*, pp. 56–7.

"it is possible to understand, to question or to assert the existence of finite things without even the most implicit reference to God". But when I say that "being" or "existence" involves a reference to God, I mean that it proves to do so when we have brought our minds to bear upon it, to use Marcel's language again, in "recollection". The experience which is to be analysed is not just what is common to all man's unconscious states but the full awareness which may be called "metaphysical experience". And analysis here means the process by which we reflectively discriminate the two disparate elements, finite and infinite, which are already present in this experience. To say that we discover God's existence in an "apprehension" of God and to say that we do so by an analysis of our experience is not to make two different claims. It is all one claim.

DOES THE SOLUTION ERR BY DEFECT, BY CLAIMING TOO LITTLE ?

It is precisely because this claim is an appeal to "experience" that it may be regarded not as excessive but as insufficient, as resting upon wholly unreliable foundations. This "metaphysical experience", it will be said, is not generally accepted; it is all very well to say that it is available for everybody and that it often exists in an unrecognized form, but the fact remains that we cannot direct people to it as evidence for God's existence in a straightforward way. It is easy for one to write it off as something merely "subjective". It is not as though we were appealing to ordinary experiences, such as seeing coloured patches. We must have some common ground as a basis, and we must reach some more solid result.

This might seem an attractive programme. But if we could carry it out (and I have argued at length that we cannot), it is hard to see why there should be any need for us to do so. If it were a matter of straightforward reasoning, everybody would have been convinced of it long ago. We cannot say that an unwillingness to be convinced is a sufficient explanation of the facts. Some people have been most anxious to be convinced by logical processes and have been obliged to recognize that they are ineffective. Knowledge of God must be an affair of mind and spirit rather than of the discursive reason if it is to be available for everybody yet at the same time refusable by everybody. We must face the fact that a "solid result", if this means a result guaranteed by some test, by the use of some accepted yardstick, is out of the question.

The root of the objection which I am at present considering is, in many cases, that general distrust of "religious experience" to which I have referred in earlier chapters. The expression has become so familiar as referring to religious *feelings* that it continues to arouse suspicion in any context. An "apprehension" of God which cannot be guaranteed by a process of reasoning is labelled "religious experience" and is written off as "subjective" because it has that label. Sometimes the objector will make common cause, unwittingly, with Prof. Ayer and announce that the mere fact that we experience something is no guarantee of its existence. Such a contention, I have argued, if it is to be taken literally and universally, is equivalent to a total and self-refuting scepticism. Unless our own experience is, as such, self-guaranteeing, we can get nowhere. On the basis of experience we can make certain moves by reasoning processes, but not the move from finite to Infinite. So the question is: have we this "metaphysical experience" or have we not? There is no ground for arguing against the possibility of it, if we free our minds from the prejudices which attend it. If it still seems to us an insecure foundation, we must examine it more closely. If there were any other account of the matter which could hold water, we should be dispensed from this task. But if we cannot produce one, there is no escape from it. We must think for ourselves, or rather "recollect" ourselves.

ETHICS WITHOUT METAPHYSICS

We now pass to the second group of objections. When we were quoting from Prof. Lewis's book *Our Experience of God*,

in the fifth chapter, we noted in passing a divergence of view
on an issue of prime importance. He considers that "there is
no immediate argument from the objectivity of ethics to the
existence of God or to other truths about him",[2] and would
clearly not accept the view here maintained that the acknowledgement of an absolute obligation is itself an affirmation of
God's existence. For him, it appears, ethics as such is a purely
secular affair. "Where is the difference at this stage between
ethics and arithmetic?"[3] He seems to think that the alternative is to impugn the motives of atheists or agnostics by denying that they have common ground with theists in moral
matters. But there is no suggestion that those who call themselves agnostics cannot perform fully moral acts. The suggestion is that those who perform fully moral acts are only
professed agnostics and are really theists in disguise. A professed agnostic may indeed object to the suggestion that he is
mistaken about being an agnostic; but he cannot object that
his moral life is being impugned unless he regards theism as
being not only irrelevant but even antagonistic to morality—
and that is certainly not Prof. Lewis's view. The professed
agnostic, that is to say, is being asked to consider whether his
concept of what theism is may not be an inadequate one—
possibly he takes "God" to mean some power beyond the
world who issues commands to us only on tables of stone and
not on the "fleshy tables of the heart"; and there are many
other possible sources of misunderstanding. Prof. Lewis, however, does not see how it could be established that such professed agnostics are theists in disguise. I find this strange. For
one thing it seems to leave moral obligation hanging in mid-
air. The absoluteness of moral obligation, as I see it, is so far
from being self-explanatory that if it were not made intelligible
by being found in a metaphysical—and in fact, a theistic—context, I should be greatly tempted to hand it over to the anthropologists and the psychologists. For if there is no answer to
the question "why ought I to do anything?" (when "ought" is

[2] P. 265.
[3] P. 266.

taken in the absolute sense), if "ought" is regarded as an ultimate datum, it is not unnatural to suspect that it is the result of conditioning processes, historical accidents which are matters not for philosophical discussion but for scientific investigation.

But it is the fact that many modern philosophers have been content with the view that "ought" is both absolute and in itself an ultimate datum. One explanation is that the Christian moral outlook is still tenaciously held by many who have abandoned Christian doctrine. They perceive a value in a certain code of conduct which they are determined, most properly, to defend. This is not to suggest that there have not been moralists in other ages who have been professed agnostics. But the "post-Christian" is in a peculiar position. He is convinced that the Christian system of thought must be abandoned; he is inoculated against the profession of theism in a special way—and he also suspects perhaps that his system of values is doomed to disappear, although he may not see that this is a natural consequence of the abandonment of theism.

PREJUDICES IN MORAL PHILOSOPHY

There are further explanations of this isolation of ethics (called by moral philosophers the "autonomy" of ethics) which are provided by the history of moral philosophy over the last three centuries. Hume pointed out that from a statement of fact (an "is" statement) there never follows as a logical consequence a statement expressing obligation (an "ought" statement). This harmless and necessary conclusion is greeted with whoops of joy by persons of a "positivist" turn of mind. The connection between "is" and "ought" is, in fact, neither a logical nor an illogical connection but a real-life one. In discovering God's existence we discover (among other things) that we are dependent on him, that the development of our powers will bring us to him and that the neglect of them will lead us away from him. That is, in rough outline, the genesis of "ought" in its absolute sense. These are aspects of a single

"apprehension", any one of which may become explicit before
the others have done so (and the others will then seem to
emerge from it), but all of which involve one another—and are
in fact present together either in an explicit or an implicit
state.

Kant rejected metaphysics (or what passed for metaphysics
in his time) and based his religious convictions upon ethics
alone. This might have led to a revival of "concrete" metaphysics, that is to say of the Augustinian tradition. German
idealism, unfortunately, moved in other directions, and the
metaphysics of Hegel, in effect, abolished personal responsibility and therefore in principle abolished ethics, although the
Hegelians in fact talked a good deal of sense about it from time
to time. I have already quoted Bradley for my own purposes.[4]

The collapse of Hegelianism led to the abandonment of
metaphysics in the English-speaking countries and to a revival
of Hume's positivist influence in ethics. A comment on the
Bradleian approach from Mr Hartland-Swann's new book *An
Analysis of Morals*[5] will illustrate an attitude common among
modern "linguistic" philosophers. We saw earlier[6] that in *An
Analysis of Knowledge* Mr Hartland-Swann regarded truth as
a matter of "dominant decisions". He takes the same sort of
line, as we should expect, about morality. In a passage about
"duty to myself" ("that familiar chestnut, beloved of the earlier
moralists") he writes as follows: "The brief and possibly un-
palatable answer is (a) that my so-called duty to myself is a
self-imposed duty and (b) that it is neither moral to fulfil it,
nor immoral to neglect it, unless its fulfilment is agreed, by
myself or the community, to be a socially important matter (in
itself or as regards its consequences)."[7] What we "ought" to
do is what is consistent with our decisions about what is
"socially important". The only "rules" of morality in general
are the decisions of the community in which we live, for "no

[4] P. 97.
[5] Allen & Unwin, 1960.
[6] P. 32.
[7] P. 72.

end can be proved to be necessarily good".[8] There is no absolute morality, except in so far as certain norms of conduct might prove to have seemed "socially important" for most men at all times. Thus the moral philosopher's job "has, strictly speaking, ceased when he has completed his analysis of ethical concepts and sentences ... it is more likely that a competent sociologist is better equipped to suggest a set of higher-order moral principles than any moral philosopher".[9]

The great advantage of Mr Hartland-Swann's work, as we saw earlier, is that it shows so clearly the philosophical bankruptcy of the "linguistic" orthodoxy which he claims to represent. There are signs that there is a growing dissatisfaction with this state of affairs, especially in ethics. Mrs Warnock in *Ethics since 1900*[10] refers to "the refusal of modern philosophers in England to commit themselves to any moral opinions".[11] She goes on to say that "even if total explanations are no longer possible, that is no reason why we should not still look at human beings in their context in the world".[12] In other words, she is not ready to return to metaphysics, but she does wish to let in some fresh air on ethics. Her excellent historical account shows clearly what prejudices have been at work in this field during the century. G. E. Moore, in *Principia Ethica* (1903), laid it down that "good" is a simple quality and that any attempt to define it commits a logical fallacy. Since he had no use for metaphysics but had strong moral convictions, he concluded that we recognize "good" by a self-sufficing intuition. Prichard and Ross, the most influential of his successors in their day, also defended an intuition of this sort. Moore's alleged fallacy need not disturb those who do not accept his starting-point, but it has nevertheless acted as a deterrent to moral philosophers, as Mrs Warnock shows, up to our day: the fear of seeming to "define good" has done much to constrict and to circumscribe our academic ethics. The

[8] P. 120.
[9] P. 163.
[10] Oxford University Press, 1960.
[11] P. 204.
[12] P. 205.

reaction against the intuitionists, who are now quite out of favour, was the theory that ethical language expresses nothing but the speaker's feelings. This view, too, in its original form, has been generally abandoned, but a distinction between "evaluative" and "descriptive" terms is still the chief preoccupation with the result, as Mr Hartland-Swann has shown us, that moral philosophy is largely confined to the analysis of moral language.

This excursus seemed necessary as some explanation of a fact which would otherwise be most puzzling: that academic philosophers, even if they are theists, may still regard ethics as a "closed shop".

THE PROBLEM OF EVIL

If we have once satisfied ourselves completely on a question of fact, it is absurd to doubt it because other facts seem to contradict it. If the apprehension of God is a fact, then the existence of evil can throw no doubt on it. Even so we should not be content with the apparent contradiction. And there are people who will refuse to pay attention to the evidence for God's existence unless they can *first* satisfy themselves about the problem of evil. This is unreasonable of them, but understandable—if one has not considered what "omnipotent" can mean.

Dom Mark Pontifex has discussed this with the utmost clarity in *Providence and Freedom*. There are limits, he tells us, to the good which God wills for his creatures, but "these limits are only the limits of the possible". For "God's goodness to creatures is limited only in so far as the creature's power to benefit from God's goodness is limited". Dom Mark continues:

> On the other hand, apart from the limits of the possible imposed by the nature and circumstances of the creature, God's goodness must be unlimited. It seems quite inconceivable that God, for inscrutable reasons of his own, not connected with the limitations inherent in the creature, should ever will less good to

the creature than it is capable of receiving.... God always gives the greatest help possible to a man in order to prevent him sinning, and to secure his salvation.[13]

This is a principle of the greatest importance, and those who have any familiarity with the literature of the subject will not need to be told that it is a principle which Christian apologists have very often overlooked. They argue that we must not lay down laws for God, failing to understand that it is precisely to safeguard God's absolute goodness that the principle must be maintained. To say, in this connection, that God's ways are not our ways, and that we must not presume to dictate to him, is to fall into that disastrous agnosticism which we have already encountered in other connections.

The evil in the world cannot be directly willed by God. It must come as a result of the imperfections which attach inevitably to the creaturely state. Dom Mark is disposed to argue, "as regards the material world, that the ultimate and highest good of the whole may require frustration for a time in the parts",[14] but he allows that "some natural evils may be ultimately due to the sins of men, or of angels who have charge of the visible creation".[15] This latter explanation deserves stressing, because without it the vast extent of the "natural evils" may seem still an unsurmountable objection. The suggestion would be that the angels, before their fall, were responsible, in certain ways, for the maintenance of the visible creation. If the created universe was to be a "reflection" of God, an adequate showing-forth of his beauty, then it must be a complete system, a hierarchy of intelligent and unintelligent creatures. Intelligent creatures must be free to choose their destiny. If they choose wrongly, if they sin, a state of disorder is the inevitable consequence. God commits them, as the only way in which his plan can be fulfilled, to an inevitable hazard. If they fail, it is unreasonable to say that he should have abandoned his plan, for that is to say that it was not worth the hazard (which we

[13] P. 55.
[14] P. 57.
[15] P. 62.

have no business to say), or that he could foresee something which was in fact not going to happen;[16] and the very notion of a change of plan on God's part is unacceptable, for God's plan is not to be distinguished from God himself, and God is changeless.

If our world is a social world, in which both men and angels are free to choose, then they may cause harm to one another. God created a social harmony, but a harmony which could not be maintained without the free cooperation of its members. Since there can be no question of his changing his plan, his creatures retain their natural powers—which they may continue to misuse when they have rejected the supernatural end for which he created them.

Two fundamental problems immediately face us: Why is it necessary that there should be such hazards? And is not God's omnipotence infringed by the very bestowal of moral freedom on his intelligent creatures? In the long run the only answer to the first problem must be that God cannot be approached except in love, and love is inevitably (for a created person) a matter of choice. A finite mind must work outwards from itself to God—it cannot be united with him indefectibly from the start. The knowledge of God arises only on the basis of a knowledge of ourselves. A mind which is immediately united to God, which has God as its natural object, would be an infinite mind. The immediate object of a finite mind must be a natural object. We know God mediately and therefore imperfectly: it is possible for us, then, to "dig ourselves in", to cling to the finite value which we immediately know and to refuse that outgoing movement to God which he offers us and for which he made us. It is only in that movement that we shall find freedom in the positive sense. Freedom to refuse is a negative freedom, and it is the existence of this negative power which is the root of the whole problem. If we say that it is

[16] It is illogical to say that God should not have created X because he knew that X would sin. His knowledge that X would sin presupposes that he foreknows, or rather timelessly knows, X as sinning and therefore as having been created.

given to us by God because he needs our freely-given love we shall be detracting from God's changelessness, his absoluteness. If we say that freely-given love is a good in itself and that this justifies the bestowal on us of the negative power, we shall be overlooking the fact that it is our union with God in heaven which is the ultimate purpose and the ultimate explanation of our lives. There is no good which could be preferred to this, and if it made sense to say that God could have granted it to us without a hazard, then (we should have to conclude) he would have done so. In fact we must conclude that it does not make sense.

God's omnipotence is not infringed by our moral freedom because it is only the exercise of the negative power which is ours and ours alone. Everything else is God's gift to us. Here I must be content to refer to Dom Mark's analysis.[17] But one point must be stressed. Our conclusion on this issue (which controls the whole discussion) will depend on what we mean by "God". If we have come to know God as the source of *value*, then we shall not find it strange that our right choices should be God's gifts to us—we are free to refuse these gifts, and they are gifts to *us*, but we owe them entirely to him and we have originated nothing. Again, if we have come to know God as the source of *value*, we cannot make him responsible for sin in any way—if it is "permitted" by him in the sense that it is an inevitable hazard, we must not say that it is permitted as part of his plan, in view of good results which, without it, are unobtainable. We must say that it is exclusively our affair and that he has nothing to do with it at all. (And otherwise the course of history will not be a real drama in which human wills are accepting or rejecting the divine will.) God's omnipotence will not seem to us lessened because he has no part in the *rejection* of himself. Sin is the most baffling of all experienced facts, but we know, if we have knowledge of God, that he is not the source of it.

But we must come back to the question: Can we really believe that God could not arrange things better for us? It is,

[17] *Op. cit.*, pp. 70 f.

for many people, an agonizing question. But the very agony of
mind which it causes is of the highest spiritual significance,
for it implies a hunger and thirst after truth and justice. I am
not thinking of those who merely rebel against the conditions
in which they find themselves, but of those who are filled with
indignation at the sufferings of their fellow-man. It is not
right that there should be suffering—or at least that there
should be undeserved suffering: this is a principle which, for
them, is unshakable. And they have reason, for suffering is an
evil, that is, it is never directly willed by God. The point is
that their desire to abolish suffering is a fact in their experience which is irreducible; it cannot be explained away by
positivist philosophers as a merely "scientific" fact; it repre-
sents an absolute conviction and presupposes an absolute
standard. Even when such people claim to be without interest
in God, the point may be pressed: what are the implications
of this crusading ardour? If they admit to an agony of doubt
then one may fairly ask them how, if God does not exist, it is
to be explained? If the God whom they desire—whose existence they *want* to prove—does not exist, it is a strange thing
that the desire should be so deep-rooted and so obstinate.
Rational persons can usually free themselves fairly easily from
desires for the illusory. Why is there all this fuss? Why can
you not face with equanimity the prospect of a world without
God?

But why (they will insist) does God permit earthquakes in
Chile, disease and starvation in the Far East and all the rest
of it? We can only give the old answers: that for God con-
tinually to upset the normal course of things would be to
abolish our world-order altogether, and that we cannot even
begin to understand the inner workings of his providence. This
is not an illegitimate appeal to mystery. It is simply the fact
that we cannot possibly be certain whether a course of action
which seems to us consonant with, or even demanded by, God's
plan would in fact, in the long run, further his plan or not.
But we must frankly confess that these answers though sound,
are unsatisfying. We can avoid a contradiction, but the problem

of evil remains a problem in that we are at this point in our deepest obscurity. What has to be pointed out is that if we reject God on this ground, we exchange obscurity for chaos and for a more inspissated darkness—for in a supposedly purposeless world we should be faced with a still more intractable problem, the problem of good. There would be justification for refusing to consider knowledge of God as possible only if God's existence were certainly irreconcilable with evil; this is not the case, and the knowledge of God is its own guarantee.

CHAPTER IX

CONCLUSIONS

A great deal of tidying-up could be done if space permitted. A discussion of this sort, in the attempt to answer certain questions, raises a good many more, and only a very sketchy treatment of these has been possible. But in the few pages which remain it seems best to concentrate on the central issues in the hope of making our positions a little clearer. Above all, in a book of this sort, the practical implications should receive further emphasis. This chapter, then, will pass rapidly in review a good many topics, and, if taken in isolation, might appear disjointed.

THE "PROOFS" IN PRACTICE

The importance of resisting syllogistic proofs of God's existence should be obvious enough in a general way. Bad arguments are very effective in turning people away from religion. They suppose that, when they have exposed the flaw in a syllogistic "proof", they are entitled to dismiss the topic of God's existence altogether, and Catholic apologists seem sometimes almost to encourage them to take this line. What is not perhaps commonly recognized is that people who believe in God are sometimes deterred from becoming Catholics by conventional presentations of the "proofs". They suppose—they may even be given to understand by those who should know better—that they must accept a purely logical process, operating on the basis of sense-presented objects alone, as the natural movement of the mind in its discovery of God, and that any sort of Anselmian "monstration" is inadmissible.

I may illustrate a common attitude by a few incidents in my own experience. A friend of mine, a priest, once called on me with a request for a cast-iron proof that we have immortal souls. He had been talking to 'bus-drivers about their souls, and they had shown a marked lack of interest in the subject or even a general scepticism in regard to it. I had to say that I thought there was no such argument (the proof from the immateriality of the soul being inconclusive), and that in practice belief in the immortality of the soul followed on belief in God, not the other way round. My friend then asked for the knock-down proof of God's existence. He had carried away from his ecclesiastical studies the conviction that rational argument was the sheet-anchor of Catholic apologetics; it had never been quite clear to him how it worked out in the matter of God's existence, but he had no doubt that it was just a question of making the right moves. What were they? Again I had to say that there were, in my opinion, no right moves of the sort which he obviously wanted, no succession of simple statements guaranteed to produce God's existence as their conclusion on pain of a logical contradiction. I then tried to explain how, in my opinion, one should proceed in the matter and ended by suggesting that the 'bus-drivers might be persuaded to read St John's Gospel and perhaps his Epistles (this was no doubt an over-optimistic suggestion; it is not easy to imagine a 'bus-driver reading St John, even in Pelican form, while he is off duty at the depot or while the rest of the family watch television). My friend was horrified. He went off in a mood of deep depression, not concealing his suspicions of my orthodoxy and muttering about the Vatican Council and the impropriety of relying in any way on "religious experience".

What happens at the receiving end when the method of "knock-down" argument is attempted could be illustrated at great length. The other day a seventeen-year-old, in an essay for me, had occasion to remark that someone had once tried to prove God's existence to him by using the principle of causality. The argument, he said, was a "flop". If it claims to be fool-proof, it always is. For until we begin to talk about a cause of being, we are saying nothing to the purpose, and as soon as we begin to talk of it we are talking about God. And there is no smooth transition, no logical bridge, from the one sort of talk to the other. It was, I think, attempting a proof for intelligent sixth-formers in the 'thirties which first brought this home to me. It is natural enough to assume at first that the abstract principle of causality is a philosophical truth which anybody can see if he has a mind to, and that one's conviction that God exists is based upon it.[1] You try to put the argument in a simple convincing form. Things change, and this means that there is a movement from a previous state of a thing to a latter state. The world has been changing from one state to another for millions of years. But there must be something about it which was always there—otherwise there would be nothing in the long run for the changes to be changes *from*. And how could the original state of the world (gases and what not) produce beasts and men? "But, sir, why shouldn't one stage change into another so that what you have left is quite different from what you started with? Like a sock that gets mended and mended until there is nothing of the *sock* left at all? And why shouldn't this have been going on for *ever*?" At this point there is nothing to fall back on except the assertion: "Anyway, nothing will come of nothing—there *must* be a source of being." "But why, sir? How can you *prove* it?"

Nothing will come of nothing, indeed, but this must be *seen*. And I found myself realizing that I had not myself become a theist as the result of any strictly logical process. In a vague way I had always been a theist, or at least I had had a "notion" of God which had eventually become more than just a "notion" —a conviction. The more I thought about it, the more obvious it became that although the "notion" had arisen in connection with ordinary experience (and was made more plausible by a

[1] On attempts to prove God's existence by means of abstract principles some valuable remarks will be found in the last chapter of *The Principle of Sufficient Reason in Some Scholastic Systems*, by Fr E. G. Gurr, S.J. (Marquette University Press, 1959).

number of commonsense arguments) it could not be laid out in a solid chain of reasonings. And the ordinary experience with which it was connected proved to be the experience of the moral or, if you will, of the spiritual life rather than the experience of external phenomena. When I said to myself "There must be a cause, a universal cause", I was simply registering the fact that my "notion" had turned into a conviction. I had simply seen that there *is* a universal cause; I had apprehended it in its operations.

Doubtless it is unwise to begin a discussion by informing someone that he has a knowledge of God, although he may not think so. We should rather suggest to him that his own experience contains some hint of God's existence, although he may not have recognized it for what it is. We should then offer him reasons for supposing that this is the case, and a good deal has been said on those lines in the present book. There is no question, then, of denying the necessity of rational processes or of appealing to an experience unsupported by reason. The point is that the reasoning must provoke the experience, but that it cannot of itself *produce* the experience or substitute for it. It is a question of leading people, by considering the workings of reason, to consider what reason is in itself, what the *mind* is. It is not necessary to use such expressions as "apprehension", "awareness of God" and so forth; it is often better not to do so. The philosopher, who wants to have a coherent and articulated account of what is going on, must use these words. Others may find it more helpful to think in terms of desire or obligation; they may be led to "apprehend" more easily if they do so.[2] There is no objection, then, to a rational dialectic which does not make undue claims and which proceeds in a tentative and human manner, not like a steamroller.

[2] Even so they will probably not use the language of "knowledge" because the knowledge of God is so different from other knowledge. And in any case they may continue to suppose that, in view of its obscurity, it cannot be in any way direct.

PHILOSOPHY AND THE APPROACH TO FAITH

The sort of dialectic which we have just been considering concentrates very often, and quite rightly, upon the restlessness of the human heart (in St Augustine's famous phrase) until it finds rest in God. It is sometimes content with a negative result (the impossibility of satisfying our desires in this world) followed by a recommendation of Christian faith as a solution which is clearly, at this point, worth considering. This is a perfectly proper procedure, and many, no doubt, have been led to faith in just that way. The sooner we can persuade people to take into account the possibility of faith, the better. The apprehension of God, I have submitted, is a summons to faith, and there can be no better way to promote the apprehension, to turn suspicion into certainty, than by an honest examination of the Christian claims. The offer of faith will then be recognized for what it is, instead of appearing in, as it were, an anonymous form (the offering, in fact, of baptism by desire). But it is in this anonymous form that it appears, presumably, to most members of the human race, and I have tried to show that the philosopher of religion is especially concerned with it. As a philosopher speaking to other philosophers, the Christian cannot claim that the apprehension of God is a summons to faith. He has his own reasons, as a Christian, for believing that this apprehension must be available for everybody, but as a philosopher he must confine himself to an analysis of human experience which leaves out faith. That is what I have tried to do in this book. It is obvious, then, that the philosopher's interest is in an awareness of God which is more than mere suspicion and that the dialectic which he employs must not stop at a mere *impasse* or a mere enigma.

The dialectic must also avoid another danger: that of pressing unduly the analogy betwen human desire and natural tendencies below the human level. If the tendency to seek outside the world for an explanation of the world or for human beatitude is discussed as if it were a "blind urge" (and this is a temptation to which many religious apologists succumb) then it is without philosophical value.[3] It is simply a mistake to talk about the human intellect as though it were an organism. Its "drive" towards God cannot be set in motion by an innate instinct but only by God's action upon it, and this action must arouse it precisely as an intellect. The effect of this action, initially, is, as a rule, to produce what has been called "a feeling of God's absence" rather than a realization of his presence, and so the language of desire is very naturally employed rather than the language of intelligence. Attempts are often made to build up a rational argument upon the facts thus presented. The result is a failure. It is true that a desire for food would be unintelligible unless there were such a thing as food, but we cannot apply this to the desire for the Absolute. In those cases where a "proof from desire" does indicate the presence, somewhere or other, of an object which can satisfy the desire in question, we shall find ourselves either pointing to perceivable facts about the universe or falling back on the assumption that the universe is a planned or ordered one. A mere *desire* for a "beyond" which is given no basis in cognition or "suspicion" can be dismissed as an *ignis fatuus*. What we have to do is to concentrate upon a "suspicion" and build on that, or rather to develop it. And we may begin by asking: can the assumption that our world is an ordered one be only an assumption?[4]

It seems desirable, at this point, to return to a question touched on in the first chapter: is an inquiry properly described as philosophical if it is bound up in this way with conversion

[3] The subject is usefully discussed by Fr F. Copleston in *The Heythrop Journal*, July, 1960, in one of a series of interesting articles on metaphysics.

[4] Why do philosophers persist in their attempt to find a rational basis for induction? The fact that regular sequences of events have occurred in the past is no proof that they will continue to occur in the future. Yet these philosophers are convinced that there are "natural laws", and try to justify their conviction by arguments which regularly presuppose it. They should ask themselves what is the source of this conviction that our world is an ordered one.

and with theology? Names do not matter in the end, but it would be deplorable to confine the meaning of "philosophy" to logical analyses and inferential processes. The practical importance of this is that the discovery of God is in danger of going by default as a subject of inquiry because the theologians leave it to the philosophers, and the philosophers, if they interpret their functions in too narrow a sense, are unwilling to take it up.

Sometimes the root of the trouble is the supposition that philosophy must be a closed system. If we are going to talk about philosophy and theology as distinct sciences—as indeed we must—then it is obvious that there is a point at which theology takes over from philosophy. But it does not follow that there is no connection between the two. The theologian continues (or should continue) to think—that is, to use the same procedures in the discovery of truth which the philosopher uses. And there is no ground for denying to philosophy the function of preparing the mind for theology by attaining to a knowledge of God which announces its own incompleteness. It announces its own incompleteness in virtue of the fact that it is a summons to conversion and in so far it is recognized as such. It carries within it the promise of a further intimacy, that of grace. And again the point must be stressed that the natural knowledge of God is a stage through which we must pass, not a state in which we remain. It is nonetheless important for that, if we are to understand this process.

Canon Nédoncelle, in his contribution to this series, *Is There a Christian Philosophy?*, remarks that "if philosophy were always and entirely closed in upon the natural order and did not encounter even implicitly that minimum and incomplete object which suffices to elicit an act of faith, it would be difficult to understand the classical thesis of theology according to which those who follow the light of their reason as best they can and are ready to obey God can attain salvation".[5] It will be seen that this is the view of philosophy which has been

[5] P. 147.

134   CONCLUSIONS

adopted in these pages.[6] This "minimum and incomplete object" is God obscurely apprehended. But the obscurity of the apprehension does not take away from the fact that it is God himself who thus begins to make himself known, so that it is not just his "existence" of which we become aware—the divine "attributes" are also found at the same time in an implicit form. Prof. Norman Malcolm has recently remarked that this is the implication of St Anselm's "proof":

> That God is omniscient and omnipotent has not been determined by the application of criteria; rather these are requirements of our conception of him—they are internal properties of the concept, although they are rightly said to be properties of God. *Necessary existence* is a property of God in the *same sense* that *necessary omnipotence* and *necessary omniscience* are his properties.[7]

THE PHILOSOPHY OF RELIGION AND THE DEVELOPMENT OF FAITH

Something was said in the first chapter about the undesirability, for Catholics, of accepting a philosophy which has no place in it for God. The Principal of St Andrews University, T. M. Knox, has a comment on the situation which we were envisaging:

> While the current philosophy obviously accompanies the rejection of religion in some quarters, in others it accompanies

[6] It derives, in the form given to it by Canon Nédoncelle, from Maurice Blondel, and for a clear account of Blondel's position (and also some very interesting criticisms of it) the reader may be referred to *Is There a Christian Philosophy?*

[7] "Anselm's Ontological Arguments", *The Philosophical Review* (New York), Jan. 1960, p. 50. In this article Prof. Malcolm exposes the confusion (into which positivist writers often fall) between logical necessity and metaphysical necessity. He may give the impression of supposing that St Anselm's "proof", in one of its forms, is a logical refutation of atheism, but he would surely agree that everything depends on whether a "conception" of God is admitted at all. If it is, then it involves a claim to have knowledge of God. But it is still open to the objector to say that he doesn't in the least know what one is talking about.

a recrudescence of dogmatic theology. All the devotees of the new Oxford movement are agreed, it appears, in allowing science to have a monopoly of the truth about nature, but some of them hold that there is also a supernatural world, the truth about which is provided by revelation. Here too the office of philosophy is but the clarification of language, namely the language in which the revelation is expressed. In either event the devotees of this movement are led by their beliefs or their scepticisms to succumb to dogmatism, whether scientific or dogmatic, or both.[8]

Principal Knox uses "dogmatic" in a pejorative sense: the point is that without a philosophy of religion theology seems an unintelligible and arbitrary business, for it is cut off from our pre-theological thinking and so apparently irrelevant to it. Unless there is some genuine acquaintance with God, the language of revelation will be analysed in a literal-minded way which may make it meaningless or even blasphemous. It might be suggested that, even if such an acquaintance were denied on the philosophical level, it could be admitted at the theological, and the situation would be to that extent saved; but in fact it is commonly rejected on both levels. Nor is this surprising: if "religious experience" is regarded as an insecure foundation in the one case, it will naturally be so regarded in the other also.

The consequences of this double rejection are serious. The certainty of faith is not derived simply from the force of the apologetic arguments for the Church's claims; it is the work of grace. That is the Church's teaching. From what then can it be derived save from a supernatural apprehension of God as Revealer, as acting in, and so guaranteeing, his Church? The alternative is to adopt a theory according to which the *will* becomes a source of certainty instead of the intellect—an obscurantist position. This is a subject which can be only alluded to here. It must suffice to say that I have defended this supernatural apprehension of God for a good many years and in various places, and that Fr Joly in his contribution to

[8] *The Philosophical Quarterly*, July, 1960, pp. 184–5.

this series, *What is Faith?*, should convince the reader, if he needs to be convinced, that the view is a tenable one. "All seeking for God", he writes, "apart from prayer is in principle atheistic. It is an absurd contradiction to set about receiving instruction without listening to it," and he goes on to speak of the "tangible transformation which the presence of God effects in our lives and how we can, as it were, verify this presence experimentally".[9] This he calls "religious experience", and he adds later: "What I have called 'religious experience' is not only the experience of a need, a desire, a thirst. It is also experience of the satisfaction of that desire, and of the quenching of that thirst."[10] At the end of the book he concludes that if we are to believe God's witnesses "his own authority must, as it were, countersign the statements of these witnesses", and this not only by the external "signing" of miracles but also by another, "interior, invisible, perceptible only to the believer".[11] Fr Joly hesitates to say simply that we have experience of God, but speaks of "the effects and signs which reveal him".[12] For even in the knowledge of faith God is still apprehended obscurely, "in the background".

"All seeking for God apart from prayer is in principle atheistic"—when we were speaking of attention to God and of "recollection" we were already using the language of prayer. Just as the knowledge of God is much more part and parcel of our ordinary experience than we at first realize, so also with prayer if attention to God is what we prove to mean by it. The philosophy of religion, according to the Augustinian tradition, has a special relevance for the Christian's life of prayer. Fr Cayré writes as follows:

> True mysticism, which is of course supernatural, is based primarily on the intuitions of faith.... It does not follow that nature has no part in it. On the contrary it can have a large part in it, whether in the intellectual or in the moral order, and

[9] Pp. 51–2.
[10] P. 57.
[11] P. 133.
[12] P. 135.

hence the value and the necessity of the dispositions which prepare for it, at least indirectly, according to the spiritual masters of all schools. The genuine (*épurée*) and living knowledge of God which Augustinianism offers us can be of great assistance here.[13]

It might be added, conversely, that if we admit no "cognitive contact" between the soul and God, we shall find it the more difficult to make sense of classical mysticism and to dispose ourselves for the intimate union with God in contemplation to which, even on this earth, we are all called.

A DUTY OF CHARITY

In the Introduction I suggested that the chief duty of charity laid upon Catholics in our time is to promote the recognition of God on the part of agnostics or those who call themselves agnostics. In conclusion I shall take for consideration a particular instance of the agnostic state of mind which is very common in our society. Recently *The Listener* published an article called "The Disappearing God"[14] ("A discussion between J. P. Corbett, an agnostic, and R. Gregor Smith, a Christian"). In the course of it Mr Corbett spoke as follows:

I have come to realize clearly, lately at least, that life is intolerable unless you recognize your neighbour as a person who has absolute claims upon you, unless you go about in the world meeting people and seeing in those people something which demands your utmost attention and all the service that you can give them. This does not mean that you have to think in terms of any philosophical or religious system so far as I can see. It is just that it is only in unconditioned service to the next man, whoever he may be, and under no matter what circumstances you meet him, that you escape from the sense of frustration and incompleteness and doubt which otherwise dogs one's steps.

Prof. Gregor Smith's reply to this may be summed up in the following sentence: "There is no theophany here—Christ

[13] *Op. cit.*, p. 152.
[14] January 21st, 1960.

is incognito and walks the earth unknown, really, and can be accepted or rejected in this." Mr Corbett added later:

> If I turn my mind round on to what it is to devote one's mind and one's abilities to another person, I am forced to say that what then comes out of myself, if anything does—and often it doesn't—is not mine to command. ... In the very nature of the case, it is something which one is given. ... I must believe that what is outside myself is good, or anyway not neutral and not evil.

He went on to say that this position did not seem to him to involve an acceptance of the claims of Christianity.

And of course, of itself, it does not. If it is to lead to the acceptance of Christianity, it must first be recognized for what it is, a suspicion of God's existence (although "suspicion" is perhaps too weak a word here, for this testimony is surely an impressive one). In such a case a direct appeal to Christian evidences is commonly of no avail until this preliminary issue has been settled. Nor can it be settled in a moment. As Dr Mascall has said, "the power of contuition [the apprehension of God] needs training ... the conditions of life in our modern industrialized societies have largely atrophied a normal human faculty".[15] Or, as Prof. H. D. Lewis has said, "Our problem is not how to get outside experience but how to discriminate within it."[16] That is what we must help people to do, and that, it seems to me, should be the chief concern of Christian philosophy today.

Christian philosophy, as Canon Nédoncelle has argued,[17] has indeed further functions, but they are not the subject of this book. Its purpose has been to argue that the apprehension of God is at the heart of any philosophy of religion which can hope to commend itself to a thinking man. And it has tried to show that this apprehension is bound up with the whole range of human experience, that is, in those features of it which we recognize as specifically human. It follows that with-

[15] *Words and Images*, p. 86.
[16] *Our Experience of God*, p. 144.
[17] *Op. cit., passim.*

out it we can make no satisfactory sense of human life. It is the only means of avoiding an all-embracing relativism. Without it the notion of truth will remain an enigma for us, and the foundations of morality will be insecure. We shall fail to understand the meaning of the moral life, and any attempt to construct a morality which takes into account only our cultural and material welfare in this world will lack any definite norm, because it lacks any definite goal. The apprehension of God is the only answer to positivism in all its forms. We must indeed be logical and rational. But logic and reason are not enough, for without vision the people perish.

SELECT BIBLIOGRAPHY

(An asterisk denotes works by non-Catholics)

In this series: JOLIVET, R.: *The God of Reason*; NÉDONCELLE, M.: *Is There a Christian Philosophy?* PONTIFEX, M.: *Providence and Freedom* (American edn, *Freedom and Providence*).

*BAILLIE, J.: *Our Knowledge of God*, London, Oxford Univ. Press, and New York, Scribner, 1939.

BOUYER, L.: *Christian Initiation*, translated by J. R. Foster, London, Burns Oates, and New York, Macmillan, 1960.

*CASSERLEY, J. V. Langmead: *The Christian in Philosophy*, London, Faber, 1949, and New York, Scribner, 1951.

CHARLESWORTH, M. J.: *Philosophy and Linguistic Analysis*, Pittsburgh, Pa, Duquesne Univ. Press, 1959.

DANIÉLOU, J., S.J.: *God and Us*, London, Mowbrays, 1957 American edn, *God and the Ways of Knowing*, New York, Meridian Books).

*FARMER, H. H.: *The World and God*, London, Nisbet, 2nd edn reprinted 1948, New York, Harper, 1936.

*FARRER, Austin: *Finite and Infinite*, London, Dacre Press, and Naperville, Ill., Allenson, 1943.

*FLEW, Antony, and McINTYRE, A.: *New Essays in Philosophical Theology*, London, S.C.M. Press, and New York, Macmillan, 1956.

GARRIGOU-LAGRANGE, R., O.P.: *God, His Existence and Nature*, St Louis, Herder, 1935.

GILSON, E.: *The Philosophy of St Bonaventure*, London and New York, Sheed and Ward, 1938.

HAWKINS, D. J. B.: *The Essentials of Theism*, London and New York, Sheed and Ward, 1949.

*LEWIS, H. D.: *Our Experience of God*, London, Allen and Unwin, 1959.

LUBAC, H. de, S.J.: *The Discovery of God*, London, Darton, Longman and Todd, and New York, Kenedy, 1960.

MARCEL, Gabriel: *Metaphysical Journal*, London, Rockcliff, 1952; *Being and Having*, London, Harvill Press, 1949.

*MASCALL, E. L.: *He Who Is*, London and New York, Longmans, 1943; *Words and Images*, London and New York, Longmans, 1949; *Existence and Analogy*, London and New York, Longmans, 1949; *Via Media*, London, Longmans, and Greenwich, Conn., Seabury Press, 1957.

*MITCHELL, B. (Editor): *Faith and Logic*, London, Oxford Univ. Press, 1956, and Boston, Mass., Beacon, 1957.

PONTIFEX, Mark: *The Existence of God*, London, Longmans, 1946.

PONTIFEX, Mark, and TRETHOWAN, Illtyd: *The Meaning of Existence*, London, and New York, Longmans. 1953.

The Twentieth Century Encyclopedia
of Catholicism

*The number of each volume indicates its place in
the over-all series and not the order of publication.*

PART ONE: KNOWLEDGE AND FAITH

1. What Does Man Know?
2. Is Theology a Science?
3. The Meaning of Tradition
4. The Foundations of Faith
5. Does the Faith Change?
6. What is Faith?
7. God's Word to Man
8. Myth or Mystery?
9. What is a Miracle?
10. Is There a Christian Philosophy?
11. Early Christian Philosophy
12. Medieval Christian Philosophy
13. The Basis of Belief
14. Does Christianity Oppose Science?
15. The God of Reason

PART TWO: THE BASIC TRUTHS

16. The Worship of God
17. What is the Trinity?
18. The Holy Spirit
19. In the Hands of the Creator
20. The Problem of Evil
21. Who is the Devil?
22. Freedom and Providence
23. The Theology of Grace
24. The Incarnation
25. What is Redemption?
26. The Communion of Saints
27. The Basic Virtues
28. Life After Death

PART THREE: THE NATURE OF MAN

29. The Origins of Man
30. Evolution
31. What is Man?
32. What is Life?
33. What is Psychology?
34. Man in His Environment
35. What is Metaphysics?
36. Psychical Phenomena

PART FOUR: THE MEANS OF REDEMPTION

37. Prayer
38. The Nature of Mysticism
39. Spiritual Writers of the Early Church
40. Christian Spirituality of the Middle Ages
41. Post-Reformation Spirituality
42. Spirituality in Modern Times
43. What are Indulgences?
44. Mary The Mother of God
45. The Marian Cult
46. What is a Saint?
47. What is an Angel?

PART FIVE: THE LIFE OF FAITH

48. What is the Church?
49. What is a Sacrament?
50. Christian Initiation
51. The Forgiveness of Sins
52. What is the Eucharist?
53. What is a Priest?
54. Christian Marriage
55. Death and the Christian
56. Christian Morality
57. Christian Social Teaching
58. World Morality
59. Christianity and Money

PART SIX: THE WORD OF GOD

60. What is the Bible?
61. The Promised Land
62. Biblical Archaeology
63. Biblical Criticism
64. God's People in the Bible
65. The Religion of Israel
66. The Prophets
67. How Do We Know Jesus?
68. The Life of Our Lord
69. What is the Good News?
70. St. Paul and His Message
71. What the Old Testament Does Not Tell Us
72. The New Testament Apocrypha
73. The Jewish Faith

TWENTIETH CENTURY ENCYCLOPEDIA OF CATHOLICISM

All titles are subject to change.